GETTING A NASTY SHOCK
The Bradford Ointment Story

Kevin McDonnell

Flashy Blade Books
Bradford

Published By
Flashy Blade Books 2012

ISBN 978-0-9574395-0-4

CHAPTERS

Getting A Nasty Shock

This is Kevin McDonnell's first book. He has previously been employed as a Journalist and English Language Teacher. He was born in Bradford.

THANKS to all those who gave up their time to help put this book together. The lads interviewed would have been on any wish list for a project of this nature. Countless individuals also provided photographs and background information but asked to remain anonymous. To those I am grateful.

Thanks also to Graham Meeson, Samantha Rubery, Wibsey Scott, Robin Doherty, Mick Jack, Rikki D, John Nolan, Ben Chang, Brookie, Muddy, Andy Larkin, Eric T, Jock, John T, The General, Ackroyd, Murphy, Macca and The Dearnley Brothers.

Cover photo courtesy of Telegraph & Argus

flashybladebooks.co.uk

Andy Naylor and wife Teresa

Coatsey

Lloyd Spencer

Andy Hindle

O_T
The Originals

Chapter One
THE ORIGINALS

ANDY Naylor is a legend in Bradford and is known throughout the country. As a young man he was a leading figure in the feared Town Boys gang who created havoc on the terraces in the seventies. It was the period of Clock Work Orange where the youth of the day replicated the anti-social behaviour of the cult movie heroes. In those days the objective was to take over the home end when City played away, and to strike fear into the lives of visiting fans at Valley Parade. One year a plea appeared in Stockport County's programme asking Andy to behave. Another time a cryptic message was announced over the public address system at Crewe Alexandra informing Andy 'his friends' would be waiting for him at a train station near Manchester. This was in fact a rival hooligan firm. His wife Teresa would often drive a van to away matches and find herself caught up in mass brawls. Andy was present when the Ointment name was chosen but soon after settled down.

Now in his late 50's, Andy has long since moved away from his active days on the terraces.

Andy
ORGANISED football hooliganism in Bradford was going on 15-20 years before the name Ointment appeared in 1977. For years we were known as the Town Boys. Newspapers have speculated and built up a myth as to why we chose the

name. Is it because victims have to put ointment on their wounds, etc? But it's all bullshit! We got the name after a Panorama documentary about Millwall hooligans who were calling themselves F-Troop and Treatment at the time. We were in a pub when it was broadcast. We had a laugh about it and chose the name Ointment for ourselves. It was a piss-take but the name stuck and obviously is still going today. I can honestly say I've never been with City when we've been done. Outnumbered many times, but never getting turned over. We were the big mob of the lower leagues. In 1973 Southport came as Fourth Division Champions and the supporters never got off the coaches outside the ground when they saw what lay in wait. The police took them back home. We always looked forward to teams with bigger reputations hitting poor times and slipping into the old third or fourth divisions. We were respected throughout football going back to the 60's but had limited opportunities to be tested. I've been going to City for 50 years now and for about 40 of them we have been in the bottom two divisions.

We did though have a disproportionately large away following and lads looking for a fight for the status of the club. We used to take so many away that hardly anybody wanted a go back so we ended up taking over most places. Barnsley, Rotherham and Stockport were good days out though.

We always had rows with Barnsley. What the older lads would do in the late 70's is go on buses early in the morning and head for a pub called The Queens in the middle of Barnsley town centre. Barnsley lads would come and surround the pub and there would be scuffles and stuff going off until about 2 pm when the special train pulled in. About 500-600 would get off and just wipe them out. Walking up the hill to the ground was something we always looked forward to. They would be pelting us with pieces of coal, potatoes and stuff. It would kick-off all over the place.

I got hit with a House for Sale sign once. We got to Barnsley really early one time and one of our lads was called 'Plank'. He got the name as he always carried a plank of wood down his leg. He was the funniest thing you would ever see at a football match. We paid in the Barnsley end and waited next to the turnstile entrance where there was this sliding door. We opened it and every time a Barnsley fan stuck his head through, Plank hit them over the head with his piece of wood. We did this until a nosey copper's helmet went spinning after Plank whacked him. One consequence of our fights with Barnsley is police horses wearing visors. A horse got hit in the face with a brick thrown by Barnsley and lost an eye. This incident made the national press and shortly after police horses nationwide were required to wear the visors while on duty at football matches.

Stockport away was a fixture we always liked. We would religiously take their end whether paying in or running over the pitch to take it.

In 1978 Sheffield Wednesday at home was a good one. Jack Charlton was their manager at the time and they brought over 5,000 fans. They were given the whole of the Kop to accommodate the numbers. Not many of us managed to get in amongst them. But in those days half of the fun was having a go when the odds were totally against you. The plan was to fight our way from the back to the front of the Kop. We all gathered at the base of the floodlight and just got stuck into the hordes of Wednesday supporters who were happy to give us a few digs back.

I remember Portsmouth once when we went in the long open end in Fratton Park. Portsmouth were on both sides of us as we walked in. We were fighting them from both sides but the lads we had in there were top class, no kids. The

Pompey lads gave way on one side and then the other. The police intervened and surrounded us on both sides to prevent further trouble but fighting broke out throughout the game.

~ ~ ~ ~ ~ ~

PUB landlord Lloyd Spencer, 54, has been going to City matches since the late 1960's. He has seen it all when it comes to football violence. The big man believes the youth of today have it easy when it comes to fighting. Lloyd says the mobile phone culture has removed the unknown. In his day you went away unaware of what lay in store. He believes football violence was more akin to that of Eastern Europe, where hand-to-hand battles are common place. As a teenager he lived in Leeds and was regularly involved in fights in his local area. His hatred for Leeds fans eventually led to a spell in borstal.

Lloyd
I LIVED in Leeds and used to get in scrapes being a Bradford City fan. Today things are nothing like what they were in the 1970's. If you did not stick by your mates you could get seriously hurt. The Town Boys were the lads who fought at City games and they were proper men. They were the local hard bastards who carried razor blades and had metal bars inside their jackets. They either worked on the doors or the doormen were scared of them. They were like the Mafia. Lots of lads went to City dressed in bother boots and had skinheads but the Town Boys didn't dress like that. They were sharp dressers. They were not only feared on the terraces but also in the pubs and clubs. We were also multi-racial, we never had any bother with the racist stuff. We always had Polish, Estonians, Irish, Ukrainians, Sikhs, West

Indians and some Muslim lads amongst us. And many of these ended up in prison for football violence. It annoyed me when Bradford Ointment lads got mentioned with the race riots as we were never like that. Some might be linked to the EDL but they are very much in the minority. No one was excluded from moving with us because of their race. We were never political. We had lousy home attendances but always had a very good away following compared to the majority of clubs in the lower leagues. We would be 78th in the football league and go down to Torquay and there would be 700 City fans there. We had a village mentality. We all knew one another and if anyone let their mates down they were not around us very long. We hung around with each other at weekends and to this day many lads from the 70's are still pals. One newspaper had us in the top ten hooligan gangs in the late 70's. Some people would have asked:

"What the fuck are they doing there?"

But anyone who came across Bradford would have understood. It was rare for an away team to bring any lads to Bradford and not get done over. At the top of the Kop there used to be a pie shop. They were very nice but also hot and we often launched them into the away fans. Port Vale supporters had to stay on their coaches instead of going into Valley Parade one time for their own safety. And I remember an escort of Barnsley fans coming from the train station was forced to turn back because of the amount of missiles being thrown at them. Both Oldham and Barnsley fans have ran across the pitch to get away from City fans on the old Kop. In Oldham's case we ran after them and they got hammered in the Midland Road too. There have been many funny times. I remember at Blackpool, a lad called Mick spotted a window cleaner and fucked off with his ladder. The poor guy was left dangling from the upstairs window ledge holding on for dear life. Whoever we played in the cup games we had massive numbers out and teams were often caught short as they expected an easy ride. Leeds were a racist mob in the 70's and 80's and they used to have a thing called the Clockwork Corner at Elland Road. Twenty of us went in there and had it with Leeds for about ten minutes before the police got in between us. I lived in Leeds at the time. In 1975 they reached the final of the European Cup. I was taken to court and accused of mugging Leeds fans for their tickets and then selling them on. Eight Leeds fans had their final tickets taken off them. I was sent to borstal for it.

~ ~ ~ ~ ~ ~

POSSIBLY one of Bradford City's most loyal supporters is Andy Hindle. The 50 year-old rarely misses a game home or away. In his younger days he was part of the Ointment and would be fighting week-in-week-out. He's been there and done it. But Andy's calmed down a lot over the years. He now organises away travel for White Abbey supporters club. Here he reflects on his younger days as a City thug.

Andy Hindle
IN the early days we would go in the home end at away matches, sing a few songs, wait for the home fans to come for a fight, and then get escorted out. Sometimes we would run across the pitch and take an end. You knew there would be a reception committee out for you at places like Barnsley and Stockport as they hated us. Barnsley fans once pelted us with potatoes with razor blades inserted. We usually went by special train with 500-600 on it, most up for it. Once in the early 80's at Rochdale, about 30 City fans got battered by Man United fans when they got off a service train. After

the match hardly anyone got on the special and waited for the Man Utd fans to come back. When they turned up they got ran up the railway lines and the United fans on the train heading to Yorkshire piled off to save themselves. Bolton once got in a part of the Bradford End, which was virtually unknown at the time. They made a determined effort to take it over. Hartlepool was also a naughty place to visit. They used to park the coaches in the bus station and you would have to walk back after the game. Regularly it would end up in open warfare with hand-to-hand fighting going on all over the place. Hartlepool never brought anything to Bradford though. It was similar at a lot of places in the 70's and early 80's. Whatever club we played they would turn out for us as we would usually have by far the biggest away following in the lower leagues and a lot of lads who would be up for a row. It always kicked off at Newport County for example. Lincoln would have a load out and it would go off every time we played them. One time we played them in a cup replay at Doncaster. There was no segregation and supporters from both clubs were all mixed together. The fighting went on all through the game. It was something you would not imagine today. In 1976 we played Oldham in the League Cup and there was a riot in the Boundary Park ground that made the national press. Chaos. The small clubs in those days just never seemed to be able to cope with a large away following and this would tend to lead to trouble. When we peaked we just had too many lads for the lower leagues. The Ointment had between 150-200 for big games during the 70's and 80's. A Dutch magazine had us down as the ninth most 'notorious' hooligan gang in England. Personally I always liked going to Barnsley, Portsmouth and Stockport. It was guaranteed at those places.

~ ~ ~ ~ ~ ~

FINALLY we come to another legendary figure. His name is Stephen Coates or better known as 'Coatsey'. To rival football supporters this menacing looking individual was best avoided. With his Mexican moustache and standing well over six foot, he looks more like a Hells Angel than a football lad. Coatsey was a familiar figure in Bradford in the late 70's and 80's and involved in many battles at football matches across the country. Now a grandad, the 52 year-old has long since left the football violence scene. But here he reveals what it meant to him to be part of the Bradford City Ointment.

Coatsey

WE had some real characters once upon a time. Peter Newby was one of them. Not a tough bloke but he had the balls of a lion. I was into Northern Soul like a lot of lads in the late 70's and used to go to Wigan Casino. It was here I met a few people who became part of the Ointment. Bradford in those days was a rough old place. Not falling to bits like now, but a tough place with a lot of hard men about. Even the coppers were different. I got a fair few kicking's off the police, but that's the way it was. I once got dragged into the back of a police van for some public order offence. It was full of coppers who gave me some right digs. They were stamping on me, the lot. When they finished they threw me out at Bradford Royal Infirmary. I was just happy not to get nicked. Times have changed. Football and the music scene is where a lot of the lads who became Ointment got to know each other and it just grew and grew. Every week we would have fights in town, sometimes with Shipley Whites who were Leeds fans. There were a few Leeds fans from the Bradford area but they were nothing more than a mild irritant. In the late 70's we managed to get a police radio off a copper and we used it week after week to find out where they were and what they knew. When you look at what we had compared to some firms like Man Utd, Liverpool, Leeds, Spurs, Chelsea, West Ham, we never had their numbers. But what we did have was we were like glue. We stuck together and never left our mates. Over the years there must have been hundreds who you vaguely remember who tagged along. But if you were not of that mind, you did not last long. You soon got the message. I just think we were a lot more exclusive than most and we were really tight-knit. There was no leader in the Ointment or anything like that and everyone was looked after. We always believed we were part of something special and we had no fear. Throughout the peak of hooliganism Bradford City was stuck in the wrong divisions. The Ointment was far too good for the football team. We were always fiercely proud of our reputation. I've been to places like Portsmouth and Millwall, who I have a lot of respect for, but we always held our own. In the late 70's, early 80's, it was like an adventure going away. I remember a Crystal Palace lad pulling a Samurai Sword out on me once looking to slice me to bits. But it was all part of the scene at the time and I'm glad I was there.

Chapter Two
GETTING STUCK IN

IT would be hard to meet a more respected lad within hooligan circles in Bradford than Chris Pickles. The 48 year-old has been involved in every major row involving the Ointment over the last thirty years. As a boy he watched the Town Boys cause havoc on the terraces and within a few years he would be doing the same thing as a member of the Ointment. He soon became known as 'Psycho' to his close pals. Chris was also in the thick of things as England hooligans rampaged throughout Europe in the 80's and 90's. Many of the incidents involving Chris are well documented in other parts of the book. But here we learn how such a mild mannered man became hooked on football violence.

Chris
IT was 1981 when I started knocking about with the Ointment and I was 17 years-old. Before that I'd throw the occasional rock at away fans over the Kop fence like many other kids in those days. I first started going with a bloke called Andy Naylor who was recognised as the main man at Bradford. He was a huge bloke and hard as nails. I'd watched Andy and his mates taking the home end at away matches dozens of times. They battered rival fans at Valley Parade too. Me and my mates used to love watching the chaos on the Kop and felt proud as they ran opposing fans onto the pitch.

One time me and my close pal Javo heard Andy and his crew were meeting in the Britannia Cafe in town. City were playing Scunthorpe United away and we were hanging about the cafe hoping they would ask us to go with them. And we were in luck. To our surprise Andy asked us if we were going to the game and when we said yes he replied: "Right you're in my van."

We were buzzing. It was pretty much uneventful until after the game when we were driving around Scunthorpe looking for someone to have a go with. We pulled in at some traffic lights and Andy told us to get out and see what a group of lads were doing over the road. I suppose this was a test. Myself and Javo, wanting to impress, steamed straight into them. But from nowhere a load more Scunthorpe appeared. Andy and the Ointment lads piled out of the van and a massive fight broke out. For me and Javo it was a new experience. Although we were well outnumbered the Ointment lads just stuck together. It did come on top and eventually we got back to the van which had a big sliding door. A giant slab of concrete followed us in. We drove off but a hundred yards down the street the van slammed on its brakes and we piled out again ready for another go. This was mad, we were well outnumbered. Before anything major happened the blue lights were flashing and the police arrived. Andy told us we could come again and we felt great.

For the first time, rather than running with the crowd, me and Javo had experienced hooliganism with the real misters who were doing it week-in-week-out. We were hooked. We mainly went to games in vans and service trains in the early days. Stockport, Rochdale, Hartlepool and Lincoln were all good places to go. I remember going to Rochdale and being in their end. I thought if I smack the biggest one the rest will run away. I punched the biggest one and the rest kicked fuck out of me! You learn as you go along.

To be honest we ran everyone in the third and fourth divisions. We faced everyone down and took over most places. Every away game we got a row because we went looking for it. And it was great in those days as you never had to worry about jail. You could get nicked and bound over at different places all over the country and it did not accumulate. Paying fines was like a routine in those days. You seemed to get to finishing one and then you'd have another one starting.

As we met the likes of Millwall, Sheffield United and Portsmouth it became more interesting. As we moved up the leagues, firms would show out for us on a regular basis. We were meeting mobs who had similar numbers and rivalries were established. Some well-known firms have made their reputation by swamping places early doors and not throwing a fist in anger. They rarely make an effort to have a go. They play the numbers game. The Ointment always made an effort whether we had 50 or 250 out. We always stuck together and that has stayed with us through the decades. For us to get 300 it would have to be a huge game. But man-for-man we have always been one of the top mobs in the country. Anyone who plays Bradford knows they will get a row. We never expect to lose.

Chapter Three

LIFE ON THE EDGE

A MAJOR face on the Ointment scene in the late 80's and early 90's was a character known as Badger. His real name cannot be revealed. He is man who has always liked to take a risk. From his early career working in dangerous construction, he moved on to football hooliganism to satisfy his craving for thrills. Standing at 6'4 and weighing 19 stone, it's no surprise he was one of Bradford's main faces. He can look after himself. But with his bulk and violent reputation, he also became a target for rival hooligans and gangsters. Badger has been involved in vicious confrontations with shady figures within the criminal underworld. Many times he put himself at serious risk, but never backed down. As a result he has spent lengthy spells in prison. The 42 year-old now lives a life on the road. He spends his time travelling around the world. He doesn't feel comfortable staying in one place for too long. This interview took place in a bar thousands of miles from Bradford. Badger features throughout the book.

Badger
I STARTED knocking about with the Ointment in 1984 as a 16 year-old. There was a group of lads from the Batley and Dewsbury areas that I first started to go around with. We'd hang about the Interchange a lot keeping an eye out for any lads from Leeds or Huddersfield coming to

Bradford for a night out. Bradford in the mid 80's was one of the best nights out in the North. It's hard to believe now. We had some proper turnouts in my time and I've seen us have 300 plus lads out. The Ointment was also highly organised. We would have lads mingling in with away team's escorts and then charge it from side streets. It would cause loads of confusion and many big mobs have come unstuck as a result. But there have been times when it has come on top too and it was all part of the buzz. I personally got more excitement splitting off from the main group and fighting smaller battles where we were outnumbered. It was the ultimate buzz of them all. I enjoyed the close contact rather than the mob-on-mob stuff. As long as I had a few decent lads with me that I could trust I was happy to drift off. I used to go to local towns for a drink, infested with Leeds or Huddersfield fans, with just a car full. Sometimes it would come on top and I got myself in sticky situations from time to time.

One time I was walking in Bradford with my then girlfriend when these five Asian lads started saying stuff to her. One attempted to grab her towards the car. I asked: "What the fuck are you doing?"

They started acting tough men and provoking me. They all produced baseball bats and iron bars from the back of a car and came towards me. One broke a bat on a wall so I sparked him. I got another and put my fingers in his eyes and he screamed like a baby. Another was moaning that I had broken his jaw. They ran off and I remember shouting after them: "Don't mess with the Ointment."

It sounds silly now but I was only 21 at the time. I found out later that a gang of Asians had tried dragging a woman into a car. I think it was the same gang. I used to go drinking in Leeds and didn't give a fuck. In fact I used to make sure I did my shopping in Leeds when they played at home. I just walked through groups of Service Crew and I would get a buzz knowing they were observing. I had the confidence that one-on-one I would have the advantage and they knew it too. One time I was with a lad called Abbo and we were in Leeds. We were walking along Bond Street and I spotted a dozen lads running through the shoppers towards us. I told Abbo to watch my back as we had been spotted. I thought this lot are not getting the gear I had just bought. At the front was one of their well known boys from Pudsey. I give him his dues he's a game lad and has a big reputation in Leeds. But as soon as he got within striking distance I right jabbed him in the face and his nose burst open. As soon as I did it a copper got his arm up his back and nicked him. Funny at the time. There are a couple of Leeds lads from the Bradford area I've now got a bit of time for. But for me a lot of the Leeds mob is full of people hiding behind reputation. In the day I hated Leeds with a passion but as you get older you tend to become less bothered. My violent reputation once led to me being incarcerated for over three years. But I cannot dwell on that and become bitter. People have used my violent reputation and my name against me. I also got into body building and abused steroids for many years. I advise people to keep away from them. They eat away at you and they used to send me mad. I'd get 'roid rage' and want to take people's heads off. They make you paranoid. I'd also taken up Thai boxing. The best thing I did was turning my back on the mob culture and turning over a new leaf and concentrating on my business interests.

Now I've moved on and I don't get involved anymore. Six years ago I was working in Leeds and I bumped into one of their main lads who I get along with. He told me I should watch myself as there were people out who would want a go. I was a bit surprised. But it came home to me that even after 20 years the mob culture made you a target for life. If you've been involved in a football gang it stays with you and in some respects you are marked. I went a few times in the Premiership and I was pulled by the police asking if I had come out of retirement. It never leaves you.

CITY SUPPORTS TRAVEL CLUB

Away to: MILKWAHL

Depart Interchange at: 9-00

Members: 6-00 Non Members:

Ring Patsy Bfd.571265

or call Market Tavern, Godwin St.

A few of the 80's Ointment before Swindon game 2012.

Chapter Four
IT'S A MEAN OLD SCENE

Mark Bowers (42)
I STARTED going to Bradford City in 1978 and remember trouble at games when we played Liverpool and Manchester United in cup matches. But the first real violence I remember taking a proper interest in, was during the 82-83 season. I'd seen City at it with Millwall and Wigan and I loved the clothes they were all wearing. I was watching blokes with Fila and Tacchini tracksuits and deer stalkers on their heads battling it out - and I was hooked. That year I saved and saved until Christmas I was able to afford a Fila jumper and a pair of adidas shoes. I got them at Top Man in Leeds, and they were the last pair of size 8's. I put them straight on my feet in the shop and didn't take them off until they bust. I loved those shoes. For someone who has not been involved in the football hooligan stuff it must be hard to understand why we always did it. But it was a massive buzz. You couldn't beat it. I lived for those days. I remember being in the Duchess of Kent and the Service Crew coming up by Sunwin House. It kicked off by the Royal Standard. There were pockets of Service Crew and they were getting done big time. As we got up to the ground we came across a massive mob of Leeds. It was like a scene out of Zulu as they all came running at us. There must have been 400 but for me, a 14 year-old kid, it seemed like a 1000. The Ointment was taking coaches everywhere and I

loved hanging around and being able to go.

In 1984 I played under Brian Clough at Nottingham Forest in the youth team as a goalkeeper. I was tipped by many to forge a successful career in the professional game. I played in the same youth team as the likes of Gary Charles. But it didn't work out as I got caught up in the explosion of football violence and led a double life. On the face of it a dedicated footballer with the world at my feet, but away from the glaring eye of Cloughy, I was a committed football thug. On one occasion Forest scouts were watching a game at Huddersfield and spotted me throwing objects at home fans and trying to get on the pitch. They told my Mother. My activities away from the football pitch eventually led to the dream of being a pro footballer evaporating. A transfer to Mansfield Town and then non-league oblivion.

Coming out of the 80's we stumbled across Ecstasy and money. You could shag women all day, drink Brandy, do what you wanted without too much effort. It landed in my lap and life just went mad for me.

The fighting at football sort of came back again for a lot of Ointment when City got to the Premier League. You would see lads that you had not seen for years turning out regular, home & away. It was like we had missed the mad old days of the 80's in the top flight so we wanted a taste of it now. It pissed a lot of lads off that the Ointment never really got the recognition it deserved. We knew that we would have been up there with any of them. So I think with a lot of people it was a case of letting these well known mobs know what we were all about.

I've been jailed twice for football related offences against Hull and Aberdeen and banned twice. My football career never worked out as well as it could have but I have no regrets. I'm doing well for myself now and I have a great family life. I play football at a decent level these days and I am making up for the time I lost messing around. One thing always led to another but I've no regrets at all. I've had some proper good laughs. I'm 42 years-old and the future is looking good. I still love the casual gear and I collect rare items. I sell them on e-bay to like-minded people. I get as much of a buzz today finding a rare top or jacket as I did when I bought my first adidas shoes in 1983.

~ ~ ~ ~ ~ ~

Dean Brimacombe (44)

WHEN we played Leeds at Odsal in 1986 I remember looking in the mirror on the morning of the match with my best gear on, thinking 'come on'. I was buzzing. That is what it was like being a football hooligan. When you know another mob is going to come and have a go and you know your mates are going to be around you when it goes off. Fucking great. What a feeling!

This match also opened my eyes. I had never seen so many different mobs of lads, from different parts of the country, supporting one team. We were fighting lads all the way up Manchester Road with different accents. I'd never come across anything like it. Being a thug also lost me my job at British Rail. We took a right mob over to Leeds in the 80's, but the police had swamped the exit to the train station. However, I knew another way out so we ran across the lines and out my way. But I got nicked the following Monday when the police came to work and told my boss he had a football hooligan working for him.

There have been lots of funny times. There was a lad I used to go to school with from Grimsby, called McCarthy, and he lived in Bradford. He knew all their boys (Beach Patrol) but I'd not seen him for years. One day we set off to

Grimsby and we decided to call for him on the way. Sixty of us turned up at his house. His mum must have wondered what the fuck was going on, so must he. We took him along though. All day Grimsby lads were shouting abuse at him:

"We'll kill you McCarthy, you're with Bradford."

I think he's still alive.

I used to live in a house with Mark Bowers, Ste Bradbury and a lad called Macca. In the late 80's and early 90's, many lads were living a life of drugs, women, beer and money. Nothing that went on during the rave and drug scene in Bradford was not known about by Ste Bradbury. He was a tough lad with a Bradford City tattoo on his neck. He was very well known throughout the north of England.

Life seemed good at the time. I was the only one in the house who had a job and most of the time when I came home from work everyone was off their heads or asleep. We were knocking off these posh birds from Harrogate as Ste had been dishing out a few E's over there. One time I was with Bowers in the Flagship pub in Bradford city centre when this big black kid called Ruthless, from Leeds, came over.

"Tell your mate Bradbury I'm going to kill him, " he warned.

"I know you're his boys, tell him I'm going to kill him." So we said if you want us to tell him, we'll tell him. We got back to the house and told Bradbury that this kid in town had been saying this and that and threatening to do him in. He just told us:

" Right we'll go in to town tomorrow to have a word with Ruthless."

The following afternoon, Bradbury came down the stairs with a crossbow. He loaded it up and then slipped it inside a plastic bag.

"Right let's go see Ruthless," he says.

We all got in the taxi and headed for the Flagship. When we walked in, there was a group of black lads sat down.

"Right, who the fuck is Ruthless?" asked Bradbury.

This kid stands up. "I'm Ruthless."

Bradbury walked towards him, pulled the crossbow out of the shopping bag and pushed it against his throat.

"I'm going to fucking kill you today. What have you been saying about me?"

Ruthless shit himself and pleaded to be left alone. I have no doubt had Ruthless got lippy, Bradbury would have let the bolt go.

After that incident no one really challenged Bradbury and he was pretty much left alone in making sure people could get hold of Ecstasy.

Sadly Ste is no longer with us.

There are loads of young lads going to City now who are under 20. There seems to be hundreds of them knocking about, YBO, Under-Fives. Last time I went to Leeds they all got on the train at Pudsey and I could not believe how many got on. Some are only about 15 years-old but they have all the clobber on. They are like what we were like in the 80's, totally devoted to it.

It's funny but in my own experience, and you hear it talking to older lads, is that in your mid-30's or whatever you realise this is what you are. You are a football lad and it never goes away. There are loads of older lads at City who went away from it all but have come back again. The feeling stays with you.

~ ~ ~ ~ ~ ~

Crowy (43)
THERE is no feeling like being a football lad. I used to iron my clothes on Thursday for the game on Saturday. I

couldn't sleep. I've never stole, never robbed, but I've been to jail three times for football violence.

I used to sit up the night before a big game going through everything in my head. I loved it all. One strange experience that springs to mind was when I found myself kidnapped by Leeds lads. I'd been out one Friday night off my head at some rave somewhere with Ste Bradbury. He knew some Service Crew kids and we got talking with them. They had a van and they were going to West Ham straight after. So everything is OK, everyone getting on. I got in their van thinking I'm getting a lift home. When I woke up I was at Leicester Forest fucking service station. I was on my way to West Ham.

We got in a pub in Kings Cross and it was full of Leeds lads. Fucking hell. I was at the bar trying to keep a low profile and I catch this lad's eye and he's pointing at me.

"You, you," he shouts.

"Bradford Ointment."

I had no idea who he was but it turned out he remembered me from a row we had with them at a Bradford Park Avenue versus Leeds friendly. I thought I was going to get battered. One of them threw a glass at me. Next thing Bradbury appeared next to me and undid the button on his shirt to reveal a Bradford City tattoo on his neck. I thought that's it, we're dead here. Thankfully some of the other Service Crew lads saw we were getting bullied and bailed us out.

I have to say when we got to London it was going off everywhere and it was a good laugh. I got talking to quite a few Leeds lads who had no idea I was Bradford.

A few weeks later, Leeds played us at Valley Parade. Three of the lads I had met at West Ham came bouncing over to me on Manningham Lane.

"Hey mate have you seen anything of the Ointment?"

one asked.

So I walked towards one of them and said:

"Yes I have, fucking here."

I cracked the cunt. I know I was with him at West Ham but fuck it. He must have been confused though. The Premiership was very disappointing. We had been waiting to get there for years and we still thought each club would have a decent firm. But in two years of taking mobs all over the country we only got involved in a handful of rows. Two of those were against Manchester United. Leeds were shit. One time, myself and Dean went with the Young Bradford Ointment to something they had arranged with Oldham. We just went to have a look but found ourselves at the front with Oldham throwing stuff at us. The YBO wanted to run at them but we just said walk. When we got to them I took a stone off this Oldham kid and hit him with it. Afterwards, they rung someone up in the YBO complaining they had brought older lads with them and it wasn't fair. There were only two of us and we are in our 40's. They shouldn't be scared of us for fuck's sake. Sometimes I do feel my age!

~ ~ ~ ~ ~ ~

Francis

THE biggest firms I have seen at Bradford are Leeds in 1986 and Manchester United in 2001. Both had massive numbers.

A lot of mobs have paid us a visit over the years but I'd like to mention two not so well known outfits. Both Grimsby and Chesterfield have brought 100 plus on occasions and that's a good following for small clubs. I got to know some Newcastle lads over the years including Brendan, Frosty and Robbie. I went up a few years back when they were playing Cardiff and the Welsh outfit had a good 300 lads in an escort which was impressive for this day and age. The hooligan mobs I respect are Boro, Millwall, Leeds, Cardiff, Hull, Pompey, Burnley, Newcastle and Forest.

My hooligan days are now gone, but I will tell you this, you can take the man out of the Ointment but you can't take the Ointment out of the man.

Been there and done it. Crowy, Sooty and Dean.

Francis

Mark Bowers with part of his casual gear collection.
Mabwindowcleaningservices@live.co.uk

Chapter Five
BROTHERS

MARTIAL Arts expert Jimmy Cooper is a well known Ointment member. He was introduced to the lads through a friend and soon became a regular face on the football hooligan scene. Previously Jimmy had no interest in Bradford City or gang culture. But after getting a taste of mob violence at Hull he was hooked. Jimmy is a handy lad and is proficient in several forms of Martial Arts including Taekwondo, Karate, Judo and Thai boxing. In fact, he ran his own schools. But it has always been fighting alongside his Ointment mates, who he refers to as his brothers, that Jimmy loved the most. Here, in his own words, is how it all started for the ex-Para.

Jimmy
MY transition from being a skinhead to a dresser came in the early 80's. Bradford had several groups who would hang about town. You had Mods, Punks, Teds, Skinheads and Rastas all wanting pride of place in the Arndale Centre where the youth liked to hang about. I would get up every Saturday morning and put on Ska music whilst I got ready to go out. As a Skinhead your boots were your pride and joy and had to be like mirrors. Stay press whites, Fred Perry, Crombie or Harrington were all the must to fit in. If you were unlucky enough to be walking through the Arndale

and the wrong mob were at the circle first you were going to get some stick. I remember one Saturday when I was on my way to HMV to buy a record I saw a right commotion going off between Punks and Mods. They were fighting like fuck and I loved watching it. The country was in turmoil with the odd riot popping up. Bradford had its own mini riot back in 1981 and didn't kick off until closing time. You can imagine everyone pissed up wanting to smash a window and get some free gear. I was walking in Ivegate with a bird when a gang of lads walked down smashing windows. Coppers were hitting anyone in reach. One lad got smacked and he lost it big time. He dropped the copper and two more before they battered him and got him in a van and that was that. When I got to the taxi rank outside the Town Hall you could hear windows going through, alarms going off, it was crazy.

Bradford's nightlife was fantastic back then. My favourite pub was the Tavern in Town (later Tickles) and it was here I met some very good friends. One lad in particular, Chris Jacques, he was well over six-feet tall and looked a handful with his shaved head and Doc Martins . He introduced me to his friends from Shipley. They all followed Bradford City and I later found out they were part of a group called the 'Ointment'. I wasn't into the football scene at all back then and never took any notice of results or anything like that.

My interest grew in football when Chris asked if I wanted to go with him to a City match because he said I would love it. I accepted and the game was against Hull City away in 1981. In all honesty the bus had a right mixed bag of lads on it. Myself and Chris wore our Crombies and Docs, looking like two right smooth dudes. I remember one kid busting for a piss so he walked to the front and asked the driver to open the doors. I couldn't believe it when he stood at the doors pissing out of the moving bus. When the bus got to Hull City's Boothferry Park the lads were all getting fired up and excited. As we got off I noticed the train pull in at the side of the ground, and it was like a stampede, lads charging down the track picking bricks up, smashing greenhouses in allotments and fighting Hull fans. I just stood thinking what the fuck have I come here for. I wasn't doing fuck all but I got dragged behind a police van and a copper gave me a crack in the mouth. I was sort of amused at how normal this seemed to Chris and the others. After the game we all just got on the bus and back home to enjoy a good night in the Tavern. We weren't in there long before everyone got talking about the day's events and a game that was coming up against Sheffield Utd.

After this I started to take more notice of the league and stuff and I realised Bradford and Sheffield Utd were candidates for promotion. My next game was at Valley Parade against the Blades. I went up to the Pack Horse where I was supposed to meet Chris and his pals but when I got there the place was empty. So I just made my way up to the football ground hoping to bump into Chris on route. On the way up I passed a pub called the Theatre Tavern which was full of Sheffield. Just up the road was a pub called the Royal Standard and this was full City. You could feel in the air something was about to happen and as I walked past, Bradford lads attacked the Theatre Tavern. I was still very much a rookie and just carried on walking.

At the ground the atmosphere was mental. I'd never seen or heard anything like it. Sirens were going off in the distance and people were walking about with ripped shirts and bloody clothes. Inside Valley Parade was fantastic. Bricks, bottles, darts and golf balls were flying threw the air. You had to look to the sky rather than the match or you would be hit by something. This was without doubt the best thing I'd ever seen, and I'm now mates with many who were in the thick of it.

The away fixture at Sheffield was on a Tuesday night and Bradford Interchange was cram packed with lads. As we were all getting rowdy and singing the police started giving hassle, pushing and shoving. This big chunky lad draped in his Union flag with Dealers on started fighting with coppers. As they tried to get him in the back of the van he was knocking them over. But there was only going be one outcome. More coppers turned up and they picked him up and threw him in the back of a police van. This kid turned out to be Steff Hirst. I found I was getting to know more and more of the lads and whenever I got the chance to go to games I would. We got promoted that season and our last home game was against Bournemouth. I remember when Bobby Campbell threw his shirt off the balcony, it was like a riot and the shirt got ripped to pieces. I got a bit of the collar. Bradford was fantastic that night. These are good memories of how it all started for me.

Danny Wright and pals before Swindon 2012.

Chapter Six

THE LOYALIST

DURING the last four decades there's been a familiar face around the Ointment. He lives by the dictum 'Never Too Old'. His name is Steff Hirst, a man with 18 convictions for football related offences.

The huge scar stretching across his face leaves you in no doubt of his violent past. It was made by a machete wielding gang rival in Bradford.

The 50 year-old self confessed thug is well known to police forces throughout the country. He has been present at most of the violent confrontations involving the Ointment stretching back to the late 70's.

But Steff is almost as well known in football hooligan circles for his fanatical connection to loyalism. He is a proud Orange man who attends many of the Protestant band parades in Northern Ireland. Over the years he has rubbed shoulders with some of Ulster's most feared loyalist paramilitaries including Jackie McDonald, Billy Wright and John Gregg. Steff was once a guest at a barbeque staged by former UFF commander Johnny 'Mad Dog' Adair. He organises and attends loyalist fund raising nights throughout the North of England.

Steff also makes numerous visits to Ibrox to follow Glasgow Rangers and has fought alongside members of its hooligan Inner City Firm as they terrorised towns across Britain and abroad. Here Steff gives a brief account of how his career as a notorious hooligan began. He tells of scrapes with rival firms, (some are mentioned elsewhere in the book), in the early years. And he also reveals how he became a dedicated loyalist.

Steff

I STARTED going to Bradford City games in 1975 after my brother-in-law moved in with us. He was a big City fan and I soon got hooked. After a while I started to recognise lads from the Bierley Estate where I'm from who were going all the time. So I started hanging around with them and getting in a bit of bother. There were about 20 of us who went regular. It was weird because in those days different estates and areas of Bradford were always rowing with each other through the week. The Bierley lot would be at it with lads from Holmewood but come City games these hostilities would be forgotten. We would even sit on the special trains together while groups from West Bowling, Buttershaw, Canterbury, Woodside, East Bowling, etc would have their own parts of the train. And then you had lads from areas on the other side of Bradford like Shipley, Bingley, Idle doing their own thing too. In the late 70's, early 80's you would have 500 on a football special and pretty much everyone would be up for it by the time you got wherever you were going. For example when you got to somewhere like Portsmouth the trains were like a coiled spring and you were ready.

I went to every FA cup game in 1976 when we got to the quarter-final. The lads who you looked up to at that time were known as the Town Boys. These were the big misters who pretty much took the home end of every club we played away. They were led by a giant of a fella known as

Andy Naylor who also became what you would call the Top Boy of the Ointment. There was no cohesive unit prior to the Ointment but on most away games you would have a good 200 who were up for it if it kicked off. In the 70's, during the Fourth Division days, we would just take over at away games. City has always had a good away support so even though we'd only get four or five thousand at home games we pretty much took 1,000 plus everywhere we went. We had that many we just used to take the piss at places like Rochdale, Doncaster, Mansfield, etc. The Ointment started in 1977 and was really a piss take of a BBC documentary about Millwall's hooligan mob known as the Treatment. I think every club with a firm started calling themselves something. A few names got banded about including The Troggs who had a song out called Wild Thing. Thank fuck we never chose that. The first time I went away with the Ointment was Lincoln in 1978. We were at it like fuck on the pitch and a Lincoln lad got stabbed near the half-way line. I remember it kicking off after in the coach park too. One of the lads got nine months jail for the stabbing incident. We had some real rows with Portsmouth in the late 70's, early 80's. Two buses of proper good lads went down in 1979. We set off on Friday night and got to Portsmouth about 5 am. Some went to the Isle of Wight and got nicked smashing a boat up. It was kicking off all day in Portsmouth town and in the ground. Some City lads were fighting in the end that runs along the side of the pitch. After the game there were hundreds of the cunts down this alley. They were trying to push the police vans over that were between us. We also had some good battles with Sheffield United during this period. We brought good mobs there and they brought the same to Bradford. I remember a copper trying to separate us got collared and had his overcoat and helmet taken off him. The lads were wearing them around the bars that night.

Another that sticks in the memory for some reason is getting to Peterborough at 10 am on a bright sunny day once in the late 70's. What seemed like the whole fucking town ended up attacking us with shopping trolleys.

Sheffield Wednesday

THE first time I heard an Ointment chant was when we played Sheffield Wednesday and we went in their end.

It was 1977 and they brought about 5,000 and they had all the old Kop. This was the biggest club we had played in the league for years. Wednesday had a bit of a reputation and it was the type of game everyone was up for. About forty Ointment paid in to the Wednesday end and met by the floodlight pylon in the top left hand corner. When everyone got in we just flew into them. In those days we were a mixture of skins, blokes with Donkey Jackets and kids wearing flares. But that was how it was in those days. One of the lads, Spike, had a metal bar wrapped inside a newspaper and it was fucking mental as we steamed down the Kop into the Wednesday fans. They obliged and to be honest it was a fight for survival as hundreds of the cunts started laying into us. Punches and boots flying everywhere. The old bill could not believe it. Eventually we got taken out of the Kop and put in the old paddock. Some of us had taken a right kicking but that incident was the birth of the Ointment. The paddock started singing it and you could see lads from all the different estates and more importantly the Town Boys. We had a laugh and created a very hostile atmosphere around the ground.

Having a go in the opposite teams end was what it was all about in those days.

Barnsley

IN August 1978 Barnsley came to Valley Parade and their fans were being bombarded with bricks and lumps of concrete as they arrived. It got that bad the police put some back on the coaches and took them home to Barnsley before kick-off.

Those already inside the ground were given half of the Kop and the Ointment climbed over the fences into them chasing loads onto the pitch. A wall collapsed to add to the confusion. The players started fighting too with Barnsley player-manager Allan Clarke getting a good whack in the face from a City player. But to be fair they were the only team that you could say brought a mob to Bradford regularly in the 70's. They would often have a load of lads up for it on the football specials. You knew you would get something when you played Barnsley. It was often fucking mental outside the train station in Barnsley. Bricks and lumps of coal would fly through the sky backwards and forwards as they tried to ambush us as we made our way up the hill to the ground. For me the police in Barnsley were the best organised in that era.

Stockport County

YOU would always get a row at Stockport as they fucking hated us. They never had big numbers but what they had were game in the late 70's, early 80's. They would play their home games on a Friday or Monday night so you would come across a decent number of Man City lads with Stockport. We'd take hundreds over who were up for it but they would always have a pop. Fair play to this lot as there weren't many teams in the old Third and Fourth Divisions who would try and have a go at Bradford. They once came in the Bradford End during a night game and 'took it'. All the lads were waiting for them in the Midland Road. That's where they used to put away fans who brought less than a thousand fans and that was often.

The thing in those days was taking your rivals end. We did it religiously but Stockport was the only team to manage to get away with it in Bradford that I remember. I know some of their lads now through Rangers games and they admit they got battered after outside the ground. Stockport sung songs about that incident for years after. Most of our games with Stockport away were on a Monday night and we would usually go on one of the special trains. We'd set off about five and be in Stockport an hour later. There would be 500 plus on the trains and we just used to steam through the cop lines and smack every cunt. Stockport would come out from the odd pub and throw glasses and then run back in and City would trash the boozers. In those days the police didn't have a clue even though there were hundreds of City fans causing trouble we always managed to get in their end. We used to just go in and chase the fuckers out to different parts of the ground. I remember one year the match got abandoned during the game and we were fighting on the pitch in the mud after they came on for a go. But Stockport once gave us a tanking on the south-coast. We were playing Torquay and they were playing Plymouth. It may be hard to believe but they had 80 lads down there. We'd been taking over their ground and regularly giving them a spanking but now they had the chance of revenge. There was only a coach load of us. There was hell on but they came out on top and fair play to them for it.

Bradford Northern
WE used to go to the rugby games at Bradford Northern and we would have some right ding dongs there. I remember having some real proper good fights with Leeds. The Service Crew always brought a good set of lads over

and we looked forward to them coming. In 1984 they brought 200 over. We were at it with them on the all-weather pitch at Richard Dunn Sports Centre. Fences had been ripped off and it was like a medieval brawl as both mobs went at each other. A good mate of mine called Wardy got his jaw broke when a brick hit him straight in the face.

What was good about the rugby games was the police were never on top of it and you could have a proper toe-to toe for ages. It was during the original casual scene too, some of our lads took the clothes and jewellery off anyone unlucky enough to get collared. It was also a time when many lads were carrying blades.

Running battles down Manchester Road were a regular occurrence in the late 70's and early 80's when Bradford Northern played Leeds, Wigan, Hull or Hull KR. It also went off big-time at the Challenge Cup semi-final against Featherstone at Headingley. They were all scruffy bastards but game as fuck.

Loyalism

I GOT into loyalism through a Leeds fan called Dave Summner who is tragically dead now after a row with an Ointment lad called Gary. I'd known Dave since I was at nursery. His parents were from Scotland and I could never understand what the fuck they were talking about. My father was a Rangers fan but I never took that much interest until I went to Dave's house. I could not believe what I was seeing. His parent's house was like a shrine to the Queen with the Union flag all over the place. I pulled him about it and that's when he started to explain the religious and political stuff. I gradually took more and more of an interest. I started going to Rangers games with Dave and became more involved in it. But sadly he is no longer with us after an argument with another good pal of mine.

I regret this deeply even today as I know if I had been there it wouldn't have happened. It started in a boozer on Tong Street after Leeds had played Middlesbrough around Christmas 1988. Dave and a few of his Service Crew pals were having a few beers in the De Lacey in Holmewood and my mate Gary was helping out behind the bar as he was knocking the landlady's daughter off.

He was wearing a vest and his Ointment tattoo was visible on his arm. When he was collecting glasses one of the Leeds lads started taking the piss and said something to him.

The thing is Gary was not the sort of kid to pick a fight with. But I know for a fact he did not want any hassle. He just told the Leeds lad to "fuck off".

But when the Leeds lad stood up Gary decked him and then ended up fighting with all of them including Dave. The fight spilled out into the car park and Gary chased Dave who ran into the road and was hit by a car and killed. I even knew the woman who was driving the car. A real tragedy.

Quite a few lads from firms all over the country know each other through loyalism and attending Rangers games. I would go over to Leeds a bit for loyalist functions and there is a fair number over there, a good 20 or 30. But fair play to them they never bring football into it so I never get any grief. We have gatherings in Bradford where we'd have a loyalist band and singer plus auctions of handicrafts and stuff like that which were made in Long Kesh. Sometimes you would have a coach load from Glasgow down here too.

Some people think we are somehow linked to the English Defence League or the BNP. I'm personally not racist at all and I have blacks in my family. I'm not a racist, I'm a loyalist.

Chapter Seven
MILLWALL AND MEATMEN

ONE of the most eagerly anticipated fixtures in the early years of the Ointment was the visit to Millwall. The infamous Panorama documentary about the F-Troop and Treatment mobs had catapulted Millwall onto the national stage. Indeed the origins of the Ointment itself can be traced back to this 1977 BBC show. In 1982 it had the opportunity to test itself against this highly rated firm.

In the lead up to the game appeals were made on radio stations in West Yorkshire for a trouble free fixture. It followed the discovery, and the reporting in national newspapers, of hundreds of leaflets in the south-east of London warning of disorder at the game. They were distributed by members of the Ointment and a previously unknown Bradford hooligan faction known as the Meatmen.

Millwall (A)
18/09/82

Steff
THIS was the game we wanted more than any other after promotion from the Fourth Division. A few days before the match I came home from work and my dad, who hated City

because I'd been nicked a few times, said:

"Take a look at that?"

He threw a copy of a newspaper at me which had a report about leaflets put up in tube stations in London warning that Bradford were coming down for Millwall. The first time we went we took three coaches. Most were Ointment but there were a few fellas who never bothered with football but wanted a row.

We left from different boozers and set off at about 6am. The tone was set by the driver of our bus who was flogging stolen dealer boots. A few bought some too. We were all pissed before we even got onto the M1. When we arrived in London at about 11 am we got off in Tottenham and went to a boozer near White Hart Lane. They had no one about but we stayed for a few pints and sprayed the walls with Ointment before getting back on the buses. We took all the pool balls with us and a lot of the lads were tooled up with the balls in socks ready for a good row. Anyhow, as we got over Tower Bridge the old bill were waiting. One got on our coach and warned us if we went any further all the windows of the bus will be smashed. He said there was a load of Millwall waiting. We told him to: "Fuck off."

And to our surprise he did. He got off and sped away on his motorbike. He was right though.

As soon as we got over the bridge and on to the Old Kent Road, the bus was showered with bricks and a load of fucking coffee cups came flying through as well. A lad called Aspey jumped out of one of the smashed windows and steamed into a group of them outside a boozer. We all got off and had it with them outside this pub that may have been called the Prince Arthur. One of the top boys at the time, Muffy, was flooring them for fun and Millwall were backing off. But soon the police had swarmed the place and half-a-dozen of our main lads got nicked including Pete

Newby, who was wearing a t-shirt with 'WHO THE FUCK ARE MILWALL?' written across it. He had the same t-shirt on a few months later when he ran across the pitch into them at Valley Parade. Sadly Pete died a few years back. But he summed up what it was like in those days. The police escorted us to the ground and put us on top of this hill overlooking the turnstiles. Millwall appeared from nowhere, hundreds of them coming from all directions. It seemed like the whole fucking area had come out for a scrap. There was even some middle-aged women shouting abuse at us. Some Millwall started charging up the hill at us and it was like a scene from a cowboy film. The old bill lost it and it was just a massive brawl. A big Asian lad who was with us called Singy got knocked to the floor and Millwall were trying to drag him down shouting:

"Get the Paki".

We were pulling him up and his pants were down by his ankles. Good job they never got him down the hill or he would have been fucked. The old bill eventually got on top of things and rescued us really. It kicked off a bit in the ground as Millwall made repeated attempts to storm our end. Loads of coins and sometimes bottles of piss were being lobbed backward and forward.

When the game finished the old bill kept us in for over an hour. Millwall had gone nowhere and hundreds were outside shaking the gates shouting:

"Let 'em out".

Eventually we were taken back to the coach park and it looked like a scrap yard. A line of coaches and vans smashed up. The leaflets had wound them up alright. A few of the Ointment who got nicked ended up having a row with Arsenal in one of the Tube Stations when they were bailed. They were all nicked again.

Chris

IT was a major thing when we played Millwall as we rated ourselves against anyone at the time so everyone was making the journey south. One of our lads was from south-east London at the time Cockney Karl. Loads of leaflets had been printed and stuck up in Tube Stations and bars in the Bermondsey area warning the Bradford Ointment/Meatmen were coming to do Millwall. The police and the newspapers got hold of it and it even ended up getting a mention in the Daily Mirror. The City lads behind it could not have wished for better publicity. We got down there and got off on the Old Kent Road. I somehow ended up on my own. As you got to the Old Den there was a dip down to the turnstiles and I could see the Ointment with loads of old bill around them. Millwall were giving it:

"Northern cunts. Where's your Meatmen?" bit.

I just walked through and got no hassle. As I got near the City lot I just turned round and smacked this cunt in the face and ran off to the turnstile. As I'm paying in I started getting dragged back out as I was half-way in the ground. The twat I smacked had come after me. I managed to get through but fuck I thought these cunts are game. It was an intimidating place the Old Den. Even the tomato sauce was on a chain. You would be on one side of the fence and they'd be on the other just staring at you. They always tried to catch your eye. They never seemed to watch the match. And if you did catch their eye it would be all:

"I'll do you Bradford cunt. Come outside now you northern wanker"

The usual shit. They were always playing cat-and-mouse with the old bill trying to find a way to steam into your end and this would go on well after the game finished too. Anyhow, me and my mate Javo were fucking about and the old bill grabbed us and started dragging us around the back and told us we were being thrown out. We could see a few Millwall scattered about outside and we thought we were going to get a proper kicking. We got out and these cunts were saying to us:

"Come with us lads we'll take you to your coaches".

Fuck that. We spotted a copper on the corner and by this time there were a dozen or so dodgy cunts behind us. We told him we'd been thrown out and he replied: "Fuck off, you'll end up getting me a kicking too."

Out of the pack one of the Millwall lads came up and shoved one of the Ointment/ Meatmen leaflets right in my face. I remember his screwed up ugly mush asking: "Are you the fucking Ointment? Who's these fucking Meatmen?" Well, of course I said: "No idea, I've never heard of them." This was the only time I can truly say I was scared in a football situation. The copper was looking the other way and was more scared than me and Javo. We managed to survive it and got back to the coaches.

They never really showed at Bradford in the early days. They once came in our seats mouthing it. They all seemed to be wearing blue Tacchini tracksuits. But as Bradford lads started congregating behind them they shit it. One of the legends of the Ointment, Peter Newby, ran across the pitch at them once. Sadly he is no longer with us.

Chapter Eight

CHAOS IN THE CUP

CUP matches down the years brought the Ointment in touch with higher division teams with the usual consequence. Violence. Big mobs coming to 'little Bradford' often ended up getting turned over going back to the early 1970's. Some of the trouble made national headlines as firms from teams such as Forest, Spurs and Everton got more than they bargained for. The Ointment looked forward to crossing swords with some of the well known hooligan gangs. Always turning out impressive numbers for unsuspecting rivals, the Ointment was determined to put up a show. What follows are some of the big ties that have stuck in the memory.

Blackpool (H)
FA Cup – 13/01/73

Andy Hindle
LOADS of Blackpool came up for this game and they were seen as a bit of a scalp for us at the time as they played in Division Two. As usual we were in the Fourth. The pre-match entertainment was a pop group who were playing in the centre circle. Just before kick-off Blackpool fans invaded the pitch from the Kop and were goading City fans from the half-way line. In those days most of the lads went into the Bradford End. On mass the Bradford End emptied and as the pop band continued to play, fighting broke out on

the pitch. Running battles went on for ten minutes. It was chaos. Three years earlier Spurs had also got on to the pitch and ran all the way across to thè Bradford End with fighting taking place in the penalty area.

Arsenal (A)
FA Cup – 03/02/73

SIX hundred had gone down by train and when we got near the ground we met 20 or so Arsenal lads mouthing it. We went towards them and they started off running down this street. Then this skinhead turned around and pulled out what looked like a sawn-off shotgun from under his jacket. Who knows if it was real or not? But all 600 ran like fuck back up the street. Fighting was rumbling on throughout the game in the North Bank.

Southampton (H)
FA Cup – 06/03/76

Andy Naylor
THE secretary of the club at the time was so fed up with the fighting at home games that he made the bizarre decision to appoint hooligans as stewards. He felt that we could influence crowd behaviour and help stop the outbreaks of violence at Valley Parade. He was wrong and I was Chief Steward. We had been fighting with Southampton from 9 am all over the town centre. There was no segregation on the Kop in those days and the fans were all mixed up together. We arrived with our white steward coats on, took them off and steamed into the Southampton fans. I ended up stopping a full beer can in my face. That was a great day for fighting and it was non-stop all through the match. We lost the game to what was an illegal free-kick

but for a struggling Fourth Division side to get to the Quarter Final of the FA Cup was a massive thing.

Lloyd

SOUTHAMPTON thought they were going to come to lowly Bradford and take liberties, but they got fucking hammered. They were up here early doors and fights were going off in almost every pub on the way up to Valley Parade from the city centre. We were fighting in the Painted Wagon and a police horse came inside to separate us. It's the only time I've seen a horse in a pub! I spotted one lad with a beer bottle sticking out of his head. In those days the Kop wasn't segregated and we were mixed in with the Southampton supporters. There was hell on throughout the game.

Brandon United (A)
FA Cup – 24/11/79

Andy Naylor

THIS game was played at Spennymoor in the North-East and was proper full on for violence. Nobody was expecting anything but the whole area turned out. Lads from Newcastle and Sunderland had come along for a row too. Brandon were a rough lot, miners probably. I think this was the first time they'd played a league club so it was a big event for them. We were in a pub having a drink no problem when suddenly every window went through. They hammered it with rocks, metal poles and bins. We couldn't get out to have a go at them and a City fan got stabbed in the door way. Inside the ground we had to share the same toilets so that became a mass battleground with the police completely losing control. There were running battles after the game all the way back to the buses. It was like a nightmare and a good laugh rolled into one. You could not identify who was looking for a fight or not as all age groups seemed to be wanting a pop at us.

Liverpool (H)
League Cup – 02/09/80

Lloyd
SIX thousand City fans travelled over for this game. We 'shocked' the football world in the first leg of the tie when Bobby Campbell scored to give us a memorable win against a fantastic Liverpool side. We lost this match 4-0 and headed back through Stanley Park to where we had got off the buses. The Scousers started coming out of the bushes at us and it was hard to know who was who. It was a proper organised ambush. Unless you heard a voice you were not sure who to hit. I remember a load of commotion in some bushes. When I went to look a City lad called Spike was rolling around with a copper. Police on horses were adding to the confusion. Everton lads were involved in the fighting too. It was proper mental in that park. A few Ointment got nicked and kept overnight appearing at Liverpool magistrates the following morning. Big fines were dished out. Peter Newby was fined £700, which was a huge amount in those days.

Nottingham Forest (H)
Littlewoods Cup – 19/11/86

Dean
I WAS on the top deck of a bus on my way to meet some of the lads and as it pulled in near the bus station I could not believe my eyes. Hundreds of Forest were walking down the side. A proper good mob known as The Executive Crew. Loads were wearing dungarees. I was sat on the bus

buzzing with nerves and excitement. I could not wait to get off and tell the lads that Forest were just around the corner. I got to The Queen pub and shouted at everyone to get out as Forest were here. There were only about 70 of us at this time but we got straight into them near the Town Hall. I think we shocked them a bit as we just appeared from nowhere. It was only a brief row as the police station was just yards away and they came running out splitting up the fighting. They were well game Forest and fighting went on up Manchester Road. After the game about 200 of them came to the Prince of Wales Pub in West Bowling. It was miles away from Odsal this pub, but also one of the places the Ointment would meet. They knew exactly where to come. We later heard that one of their lads had been working up here and had sussed things out. It went off big time with all the City lads emptying a wagon full of scaffold poles to use as weapons.

The trouble made the national newspapers the following day.

Francis

TEN of us were on a bus leaving town when we noticed a group of 15 Forest lads walking up the road. We got off the bus and ran towards them. As we got closer they looked like a good set of lads. We ran at them and some of them went into their pockets and produced yellow jiffy bottles. They had ammonia in them which they squirted at us making us back off. One of our lads got it straight in the face. We went back at them and it was a great brawl for a good five minutes.

It stopped when Bucker (R.I.P.) nutted this lad. The sound was mental, enough to make us all stop. This Forest lad didn't know what hit him, he stayed standing though, but had no idea who or where he was. His mate dragged him away jogging off up the road, with the rest following, we were satisfied enough.

Later a Forest van got overturned and set on fire.

Telegraph & Argus:
"Two police vans were stoned and a Nottingham Forest supporters' van was overturned as football hooligans went on the rampage in Bradford last night. Fighting broke out near the city centre shortly after 6 pm and a van hired by Forest supporters travelling to Bradford was pushed over. The vehicle caught fire causing £1,000 of damage. At 7.30 pm a group of 200 youths began fighting in West Bowling. A police dog van was stoned and one youth was taken to hospital after a bottle hit him on the head. Shortly after 9.30 pm a police task force van was stoned on Mayo Avenue and fighting broke out again between 200 rival fans in Manchester Road. Despite the trouble police said it had been a relatively quiet night."

Everton (H)
FA Cup – 31/01/87

Jimmy
THE usual big drinkers were in The Queen at opening time for this one. Myself, Big Ginner, Bazza, Gilly, Reynolds, Cough, the Dearnleys and Chris Pickles. It was a rare thing if any of the mentioned weren't there at opening time. Ginner would usually turn up from the casino next door always moaning he was skint but he always had enough for a beer. We all looked after each other and my mates were like brothers to me. Anyway it wasn't long before General came running in saying Everton were on the platform in the Interchange. When we got outside loads of fights were going off up and down the street. Fucking great. It was

pretty awkward trying to judge numbers, and who was who, with people shopping and stuff. But you could see lads having it all around the junction of Hall Ings and behind the Town Hall. I soon found out who Everton were though when this loud mouth midget splattered my nose and put me on my arse: "Come on then wheeere Everton," the little cunt was shouting as I tried to get to my feet. As I got up I saw the fella laying into another City lad. This cunt was going to be mine. But just as I was about to punch the cunt into next year I found myself on my arse again with a fat bloke on top of me. I was getting done by Laurel & Hardy and this bastard ripped my brand new leather jacket too. A copper with a dog got fatty off me and everyone began to disperse. It was a good do this. There must have been 80 plus Everton and about the same of us. No one got the upper hand but I know some Scousers will have had sore heads, as for whatever reason, a load of ours had coshes. Just before kick-off we were having a few beers outside the Belle Vue pub in Manningham when we noticed this group of lads heading to the ground. Bang in the middle was the fat cunt who was on top of me earlier. We fired into them outside a second-hand shop with old tables and chairs flying in all directions. I focused on fatty. I ran over, dropped my shoulder, and let my left hand go quicker than a missile. I caught the cunt right on the button but he never even blinked. Thank fuck my mate Matt smashed him over the head with an antique table and put him down. Inside the ground we found out Everton lads were paying in the Bradford Kop. We waited for them to come in, followed them until out of sight of the police, and then battered the cunts. I was too enthusiastic and headed for one who was just paying in. I got him trapped and preceded to punch fuck out of him in the turnstile, it was pretty difficult holding the bars and trying to aim but I gave him a few cracks as well as breaking my finger in the process. After the game, which we lost 1-0, we went back up towards the Belle Vue pub and found a mini-bus of Everton lads in the petrol station next door. It got flipped over on its side with the Everton lads still inside.

Luton (A)
League Cup Quarter Final – 19/01/88

Dean

SCARIEST experience I've had was at Luton. It was the first time they had allowed away fans back at Kenilworth Road since Millwall had wrecked it. We had to have these plastic ID cards to get in the ground. Two coach loads, vans and cars set off early and we were camped in Luton by 2 pm. There were City fans all over the town and in the boozers. It was like a carnival atmosphere and although we had a good 150 lads out we got no trouble all afternoon. By 6 pm we were all over the place and had split into several groups. Eventually some of ours bump into Luton's firm known as the Migs and had a do with them. These were mostly white kids and our lot soon had them on their toes. But about 20 of us had gone wandering around Luton and we were pretty pissed. We ended up behind these flats in this predominately black area near the town centre. Word must have got about Bradford were about and we walked right into an ambush. All off a sudden these black lads appeared from nowhere, from car-parks, pubs, flat stairwells, everywhere. To add to the confusion they were blowing whistles. We were fucked. The first few came at us and we managed to back them off but we were in serious shit as it seemed the whole area had come out for us. I'd taken some young lads with me from where I live for the experience and I had led them into hell on earth. I could not just look after myself here. I've never been happier to see a cop van screech to a halt. The police got out and tried to protect us but this lot were having none of it. One big cunt wearing a wax jacket grabbed a copper by the throat and pushed him aside. The police bottled it. We were on our own. By this stage we knew they were tooled up as well. They had sticks, axes, knives, rubber aerials from cars and one fucker even had a ball and chain swinging round his head. I thought they were going to kill us. We were fighting for our lives. A lad next to me called Matty was having a real do with them and had just thrown a traffic cone into a load of them when I saw a lad just run up and slice him across the back with a blade. I remember him shouting:

"They've got me."

It was desperate. We just had to run as fast as we could with what seemed like the whole black population of Luton on our tail. We got to this line of taxis and jumped in. We pulled one lad through the window of our taxi just in time as the back window was clattered as we drove off. We only got a hundred yards up the street when the taxi driver stopped to check the damage to his car. We were shouting at him to fuck off but the daft cunt got out. He soon got back in again when he saw what was running up the street. He was mounting the pavement and running red lights to get away. The whole experience was chaotic and the only time really I've thought my life was in real danger. I got knifed against Bristol but I never saw it coming. At Luton the whole nightmare was staring me right in the face. If any of our lot had gone to ground they would have been killed. I have no doubt about that. Matty survived his stabbing but got a shed load of stitches. During the game we smashed bits of their stand up and went on to the pitch at the end. Some lads were swinging on the goal posts and a copper got his shoulder broke after he was hit with a lump of concrete thrown by City fans. We left the ground from the small end behind the goal. We had smoke bombs going off and stuff. Mind you they were useless. I threw one near the ground and it never went off. A fucking car ran over it and it still never went off. Luton was nowhere to be seen but some of the houses adjacent to Kenilworth Road had windows smashed. The trouble made the national newspapers the following day. We never realised Luton was so rough. Dodgy place that.

Daily Mirror:
"Luton's fan ban backfired last night when they relaxed the rule for the Littlewoods Cup Quarter-Final with Bradford City. A policeman was hit by flying concrete from the Bradford section of the ground and taken to hospital with a suspected broken shoulder. And earlier, in the town centre, trouble flared as a Yorkshire fan was stabbed in a skirmish. Chief Supt Glyn Spalding in charge of police operations at the ground admitted: "It has been a disappointing night and we will have to analyse what we do for the next round. We had 43 men on duty for Saturday's match with Derby and increased that to 198 tonight, more than four times the normal number. The whole of the town had benefited from the ban on away supporters.""

Tottenham (H)
FA Cup – 07/01/89

Mark
AFTER the game 200 Ointment were hid down a back street near the old Mayflower Club on Manningham Lane. We had won the game 1-0 and the Yids had brought a very good mob. It had gone off before the match between small groups. Most of the Yids were in the main stand where the

away fans had been allocated two blocks. We knew Spurs would be looking for a pop after the scuffles that took place before the match. Everyone had left the ground early and made their way to the pre-planned meeting place. Despite being only a few hundred yards from Valley Parade the police had no idea where the Ointment had gone. The narrow street was heaving. Within a few minutes of the final whistle, as expected, one hundred plus Yids came walking towards Manningham Lane. Some of the lads were shouting for everyone to wait until they got closer. When they got within 50 yards everyone just ran out of the dark alley and into the approaching Spurs mob. They were taken totally by surprise both by the rapid assault and the numbers we had. But fair play to them they had a go back despite coming up the hill. Within seconds the old bill began to run up from the ground as a single dog handler struggled to keep both groups apart.

Badger
SPURS brought a really good mob to us for this match. I remember before the game a couple of coaches of lads under police escort on Manningham Lane. They were trying to take the piss by waving their £50 notes as they went past as if we were paupers. We had loads out for them after the game and they got it. What sticks in the mind about this was that I felt pissed off with some of our own lot. They had collared this Spurs lad and dragged him up a side street. When I went to have a look they had stripped him down to his underpants. His leather jacket, his trainers, jeans, everything had gone. I did not want to be part of that. In fact I was appalled.

Tottenham (A)
Carling Cup – 30/10/90

Steff
TWO coach loads of decent lads went down to London for this night game. We were expecting a welcoming committee after what we had done to them at Bradford. On the way we stopped off at St. Albans for a drink and we hung about there for a few hours. All sorts of things were going off including a camping shop losing a few of its expensive jackets. The drivers were keen to get us out of there early as they said the traffic getting into London would be horrific. And by this time the old bill were onto us. So we left St Albans about 3 pm and got to North London in a couple of hours. One of the lads had brought distress flares and these huge rocket fireworks. We went straight to a boozer the Yids were supposed to go drinking in not far from the ground. But there were only a few in so we left them. Some of the lads smashed up the Spurs shop near the ground so the police were all over the place. There was still no sign of their mob so we went looking for them up Tottenham High Road. As we were walking up one of ours came running back saying he'd just spotted the Yids heading our way. There was a good 100 plus of us and everyone was up for it. We hid down this side street and waited for them to get closer before we gave it to them. This was exactly the same tactic we used against them in Bradford in 1989.It was pitch black and the adrenalin rush was immense. We were right on the patch of arguably one of the best mobs in England and we were going to give them the shock of their lives. About 50 of them came bouncing down with a swagger and some were jogging so they knew we were about. As half of them came past we let out a huge roar and piled out of this alley. Straight away a flare was fired into the middle of them and split the Yids in

two. Most of them ran straight away with ours on their tail. Some stood and had a pop but they got hammered. Fireworks were bouncing off buildings and buses, it was fucking great. With the sounds of screaming, shouting and fireworks, came the sound of police sirens. With blue lights flashing we jogged back to the ground. Job done. We came down to smash the Yids and did it. In those days a football ban only meant you could not enter the stadium so Crowy, who was on a ban, stayed outside and got talking to some of the Spurs lads. They were livid at what had happened. They were offering him out one-on-one and that type of thing. But it would have been suicide had he gone on a walkabout with any of them. Besides, that's not the game we played. One lad was telling us his dad knocked about with the Kray twins. Well done.

They had their chance and ended up chased on their own manner. Some admitted that they half expected us to show and had a good few lads out but only properly got together after we had done them. We lost the game 2-1, and after, a load of Yids were hanging about outside the ground and trying to get us to head towards Broadwater Farm estate which was a dodgy place. A few did and got nicked with old bill swarming all over the place.

Crowy

WE'D go everywhere in the country and never felt worried. We knew we had a top mob. I remember going to Tottenham and they got the shock of their lives. They were panicking like fuck. We had them all over. After the match speaking to some of their lads you could see they were in shock and embarrassed. They underestimated us and paid for it. I was banned from football at the time but in those days you could still hang about outside the ground. Some of the Yids were keeping me company and had a pop when they could. Tottenham show us respect now.

Chapter Nine
YOUR MATE STABBED ME

Bristol City (H)
18 /01/ 89

THIS was the Quarter Final of the League Cup and a big
occasion for two success starved clubs. Bradford City was
in the old Second Division and Bristol City in the Third. A
full house was present at Valley Parade with most fully
expecting the home side to progress. However, three
thousand supporters from Bristol had other ideas and it was
they who went home happy after defeating Bradford in a
shock 1-0 victory. Among the impressive away following
were 100 plus members of City Service Firm (CSF). This
group had a bit of a reputation in the south and had rows
with Millwall and Portsmouth around that time. They had
never showed up in Bradford before but the Ointment
expected something. Loads had met in city centre pubs from
early afternoon but Bristol were nowhere to be seen. Some
thought they had bottled it. But the picture changed nearer
the ground as the 7.45 pm kick-off approached. Small
pockets of Ointment lads were having it with the CSF along
Manningham Lane. And a few running battles took place
outside the ground. But nobody really knew how many
Bristol had brought as it was dark, and the skirmishes were
brief. After the game a group of Ointment's main lads

clashed with a 100 strong CSF mob in Cornwall Terrace, just outside the ground. During the disturbance, Dean Brimacombe, 19, was almost killed after being stabbed in the back. The knife blade missed piercing vital organs by millimetres.

This is how the Telegraph & Argus reported it:

"He was attacked during a night of violence before and after Bradford City's Littlewoods Cup defeat by Bristol City. Fights broke out before the game and police made 17 arrests. Twenty minutes before the match, mounted police were called in to separate brawling thugs. There were running fights with dozens of rival fans punching and kicking each other. They were running amok and people queuing innocently to get into the match had to get out of the way of the gangs.

Mr Brimacombe recalled: "Bristol City fans started coming towards us, shouting abuse and taunting us. We carried on walking but one lad jumped on me so I retaliated and swung him to the ground. The next thing I knew I felt a warm, sharp pain in my back. I've never felt pain like it. My friends ran to get me an ambulance and by the time I got to hospital the blankets I was in were soaked in blood."

He was treated for a four inch deep wound in the right side of his lower back.

Mr Brimacombe said he was declining an offer of a free ticket to Bristol City's cup semi-final at Nottingham Forest."

Dean

BEFORE the game around the ground they had been taking the piss really. Bristol had been having it with pockets of our lot and they had come out on top. But they'd not bumped into us yet. Before the game we had a word with a few of them as they were going into the ground and told them where we'd be waiting after the match finished. We were at the edge of Cornwall Terrace which is a street that runs off Valley Parade. Everyone was pissed off because Bristol had been getting results on and off the pitch. We were ready as they came along the street. It was dark but you could see they had decent numbers. Both sets of lads just walked towards each other and I said to myself "These fuckers are up for it." It went off and neither of us gave an inch. I was getting the better of this kid who grabbed me and I threw him to the floor. I bent over and then I felt this pain. I knew straight away that I'd been stabbed. It was a weird feeling as it felt like the knife was still inside me. The kid I was fighting with was on the floor and I punched him in the face and said: "Your fucking mate's stabbed me." My pal Tommy said to me straight away: "You're not going to die," and stuff like that. But I knew by the look on his face it was bad. I went to the ground and St. John's Ambulance staff had a look and said I had to be taken to hospital quick. When I got to the Bradford Royal Infirmary I was given six pints of blood. I'm saying to myself: "I'm not going to die" and trying to keep steady. I'm half conscious when two mates Macca and Morelly come bouncing through the ward telling me they'd just had Bristol all over. What I didn't know at the time was doctors were only giving me a 50-50 chance of surviving. I was dying and all the lads wanted to tell me was they had just fucked Bristol.

I was in intensive care for a week. I got 36 stitches on the inside and 12 on the outside. The knife was only a couple of centimetres from coming out of the other side. Now it would be about six inches but I was a thin lad once-upon-a-time. I was lucky. Joe Jordan, who was the Bristol manager, sent me tickets to see them play but I ripped them up. I even had ex-birds coming to see me. They were good

Bristol City and fair play to them. All together I'd say they must have had 150-200 lads out. A few months later the police wanted me to go to court to see if any of the Bristol lads arrested on public order offences was the one who knifed me. I didn't see who stabbed me and even if I had I wouldn't have said anything. Loads of them had been nicked.

Mark

AFTER the game about a dozen of us were hanging about near the back of the Bradford End waiting for Bristol to come out and to see which way they went. But we didn't know they had already left the ground. Loads of them just started pouring round the corner. We went forward and I remember getting put on the floor. There was a wall of the cunts coming at us. In the mayhem I'm on the floor being booted in the head by a mate. So I'm screaming at him to stop kicking me and I'll never forget what happened next. This Bristol lad came out of the crowd wearing a khaki jacket and an Aquascutum scarf round his face. Like slow motion I saw him pull out this blade with a big handle on it. By this time Dean is next to me on the floor and I saw this lad just stick the knife into him. He then just disappeared back into the crowd again. I was lucky as it could easily have been me who got it.

Crowy

WE were having do's with them around the ground and we were surprised how many lads they had brought. We'd never had anything with this lot in the past.

We were on Manningham Lane when we heard Dean had been stabbed. Everyone was well up for it after hearing that. About an hour after the game we got word that Bristol were in the Craven Heifer Pub on Manchester Road, which is about three miles from Valley Parade. Everyone just started flagging taxis down and headed up. We got there and someone checked the tax discs of mini-buses and vans in the car-park. It confirmed they were from Bristol. One fat cunt came out of the double doors of the pub and he got bottled straight in the face. The rest inside didn't want to know and ran upstairs and behind the bar. The police were there in minutes but not before the Bristol transport was smashed to pieces. We all dispersed when the police came but we spotted more Bristol filling up with petrol nearby. I walked across the forecourt and they thought I was one of them. This lad at the pump said something so I decked him. Loads of Ointment were getting out of taxis and off buses at this point. All I can say about what happened next is Bristol caught in the petrol station were left traumatised. Everyone was going mental. Some thought Dean had been killed and any Bristol hanging about Bradford that evening were going to get a hiding.

Chapter Ten
BIG REPUTATIONS

ALL of the major clubs in the country had decent sized firms who forged reputations home & away from the late 70's onwards. The old first and second divisions had gangs of hooligans almost as well known on the terraces as the teams they supported. As Bradford City became more successful, the Ointment started to clash with these groups on a more frequent basis.

Middlesbrough Frontline
Middlesbrough (H)
29 /08/ 84

Jimmy
IN my opinion Middlesbrough are the best of the lot to come to Bradford. They come looking for it. This was a League Cup match and I managed to get off work early and headed into town to meet the lads at the The Queen. I knew Boro were in Bradford early doors because in the afternoon two mini-buses of lads had stopped at a petrol station where my girlfriend worked earlier in the day. They had also been spotted drinking in the Ring o' Bells in Eccleshill. But we couldn't find them anywhere in town. A common fault of ours is breaking up when nothing occurs and this was no different. As we got up near the ground there were maybe

20 in our group but still no sign of Boro. We went for a pint in the Belle Vue which was a pub with strippers and full of scarfers. But as I walked in I spotted a lot of unfamiliar lads in smart gear. It was Boro. We went back outside and Boro followed, fucking loads of the cunts. They came straight at us and we were all fighting like hell at the top of Valley Parade. Lucky for us some more of our lot appeared because we were well up against it. I got caught with a punch to the head and my legs buckled. I was on the deck getting the fuck kicked out of me when a lad called Duffy(RIP) helped me out. Everyone was spread about hitting all and sundry, lads getting knocked down, picked back up, fucking magic. The coppers arrived and were hitting whoever they thought was involved. Boro had all grouped up just outside the ground and there was a good 100 of them. The coppers then marched them into the ground. Fifteen minutes before the end of the match we were winning 2-0, Boro, who were in the away section of the Kop, started to make their way to the exit. We saw them leaving and followed, but the old bill were on top of things and got Boro out of town straight away.

Stoke City Naughty Forty
Stoke City (H)
(Elland Road)
01/09/85

Steff
STOKE have never showed up in Bradford but they brought a very good firm for this game in Leeds. We walked from the city centre and had not seen a thing until we got to the ground. There were only about 50 in the group I walked up with. Then we bumped into them. There must have been 120 in Peacock Pub car park opposite Elland Road. They

hardly had any kids with them either. Stoke had brought a right firm and we had just walked into it. They came running over at us and although we had a go, we got done. They were all over us and I remember as it's going off another lot piled out of the back of a removal van. It came on top and we had our backs against the wall until the police on horses moved in. Inside the ground we were all sat in the main stand and Stoke came in. At the front of them was a Service Crew lad called Browny. He was trying to get them to have it with us and they charged us. This time the numbers were more even and it was toe-to-toe for a few minutes. As the police moved in we carried on fighting by the tea bars at the back of the stand. Eventually the police broke it up and took the Stoke lads out of the seats along with Browny. We were at it again after the game in The Peacock car-park. It was a brief toe-to-toe but one funny thing I remember was a dog handler let his German Shepherd loose and it was going mental in the back of one of the Stoke vans. I give Stoke a lot of respect for the mob they brought that day.

Aston Villa C-Crew
Aston Villa (H)
28 /11/ 87

A FEW of us were in The Queen as usual when a kid came in and said a group of Villa were in the Birdcage Bar inside the train station. We went up and rest assured there was a few Villa in there. We smacked a few but they didn't stand for a minute and ran like fuck. There was not much happening before the game and to be honest we were left disappointed at Villa's no show. One of our lads had come across two mini-buses parked up at the bottom of Thurnscoe Rd, near the ground with Birmingham newspapers on the seats. So after the match 20 of us went back to the vans. It was dark and as we got near the vans a load of Villa appeared from one of the side streets. There was fucking loads too and certainly more than two van loads. We found ourselves up against it and to be honest I thought we'd had it. I recognised the cunts who ran out of the bar at the train station among them. I picked a piece of scaffold post up that was on the floor and I just starting swinging the fucker to keep them at bay. Thank fuck the old bill arrived on horses as we were getting swamped.

Aston Villa (A)
02/05/88

Badger

THIS was a Bank Holiday Monday fixture and the weekend before about 50 of us had gone to Rhyl in vans where there had been some trouble with Man City lads. Loads of acid had been taken and a lot of people were off their heads. City took 9,000 to this game and if we had won we pretty much would have secured a spot in what is now the Premier League. We had all lost each other coming into Birmingham and our mini-bus was on its own. Before kick-off two coaches of Ointment had it with Villa in the car park near the ground. This was a lot of the older lot and some major heads. Villa had come bouncing over when the coaches pulled in but were ran back. One Villa lad took a metal bucket of piss in the face knocking him out. But there were sixteen of us not knowing where the fuck to go so ended up in the home Holte End which was heaving. Despite being maybe 10,000 in this huge terrace, we eventually got sussed and escorted out of the ground. We ended up hanging about outside until the end of the game. It was then we spotted Villa's lads. There were loads of them, maybe 200 plus. We kept our heads down trying to make our way back to the mini-bus but then for some mad reason the old bill pushed us across the road into the Villa mob. They were onto us straight away and started laying into us as more Villa at the front came back to have us. We were backed up against a wall with Villa lads actually falling over one another to get involved. We just swung like windmills to keep them at bay. The sheer numbers they had went in our favour as they were finding it hard to get at us. We were fighting for our lives against this huge swarm. The police realised what a fucking mess they had made and started beating Villa back. They then formed a line between us and Villa before more coppers arrived.

Steff
TWO coach loads of us set off from the Red Ginn. We got in to Aston and stopped at some traffic lights. Loads of Villa lads were outside a pub and they clocked us. They started slinging stuff at the coaches including a fucking champagne bottle. So we all piled off the coaches from the back and front and we were at it on the street. On one of the coaches was a metal bucket that you find behind the bar in pubs. The lads had been using it to piss in. This Villa lad at the front comes forward and a lad from West Bowling swings the bucket and smashes it right in his face. He was out cold with piss all over him. I thought the lad was dead. The old bill arrived and there is a fuss about this Villa kid who was out cold for what seemed like ages. We all get put back on the buses and these Villa lads got on the coach with the old bill. They are looking for this West Bowling lad. But the funny thing about it was the only lad not to get off the bus was Burkey because he had a broken leg. Yet he was the one they pointed out and he got nicked. After the game we were at with them again but the police were on top of it. Later Burkey got out without charge.

Newcastle United Gremlins
Newcastle United (ACID)
14/ 10//89

Dean

THIS trip has to go down as one of the most mental away days ever. We set off from the Red Ginn on a double decker. Most of us had been out the night before and there were loads of Purple Ohm acid tabs floating about. I'd say most of us were off our heads before we set off. And to add to the madness, for many on the bus, it was the first time they had taken acid. A few had never even taken drugs before. But here we all were dropping LSD for fun. We got to Durham and stopped off for a bit. It was complete chaos with little groups of us walking about off our nuts. One lad called Baz, had a bad turn and froze in the shopping centre. The kid was out of it. He got paranoid about the escalators and refused to go down them. He was shouting for an ambulance and eventually someone dialled 999. Ten minutes later he was taken away by paramedics and whisked away in an ambulance. When we got to Newcastle we bumped into some of the Gremlins near the ground. You could see they were surprised to see us and they didn't seem to have many out. Thank fuck as we were in no state to have a row. We legged them around the ground and then got wrapped up by the old bill. The police lined us up and started filming us outside the stadium. This Inspector warned us that if any of us were drunk we would be arrested as we went inside the ground. We were Ok though as we were just off our fucking heads on LSD. In the ground to the seats on the right, you could see the Newcastle mob forming in numbers. Word had obviously gone round that we had brought a decent firm up. After the game the police tried to take us to the train station as they thought we had come by rail. A few Newcastle were gobbing it but nothing happened. We got to our coach and as we headed south on the A1, someone spotted Baz hitching a lift on the side of the road. He had signed himself out of hospital. The driver would not pick him up but was persuaded to stop and Baz came running down the road with eyes sticking out of his head. Later that night he dropped another Purple Ohm and smashed his flat up.

Newcastle United (H)
21/03/90

Chris

THIS is where I witnessed one of the best one-on-one fights I've ever seen.

There was about fifty of us by the Mayflower Club on Manningham Lane waiting to ambush Newcastle's Gremlin firm who had parked near the ground in vans and mini-buses. We spotted them coming towards us a few minutes after the final whistle with no police escort. We charged into them from the side as they walked past us. What followed was a cracking fight with both sets of lads going for it. But after a minute or two everyone seemed to part and watch what was happening on the pavement. One of our lads from West Bowling, and this Geordie kid, were proper smacking each other with everything they had. One would throw a haymaker, and then stand back while the other did the same. It was just like a scene from a wild-west bar fight. Even some coppers stopped to watch it as they took it in turns to smack one another with all they had. It took a police horse to separate them in the end.

Wolves Yam Yam Army
Wolves (H)
13/01/90

Francis

WHEN we were on the ship Tor Britannia, the one that was turned back on route to Sweden, we met some lads from Wolves. They had been getting a hard time from Boro's firm onboard. We looked after them and ended up giving Boro a kicking. Ten or so of us were in The Queen Bar the morning of this game and about 40 Wolves turned up. They were a mixed race bunch and one of them was wearing a Turban. They were looking for Gervais, he had knocked a Boro lad out for picking on some these Wolves kids and they wanted to buy him a pint. We were being alright with them but Gervais wasn't about and as the day wore on tensions started to surface. One of the Wolves lads, not the one with the Turban, had actually spent his childhood in Bradford so he knew his way about. But as more and more of our lot started to show up it was on the cards such a large group of Wolves would get targeted. It did eventually kick-off in Ivegate and these lads gave a good account of themselves but they got done. Even the local coppers laid into them with truncheons. I didn't get involved and I felt bad about it but they took a risk coming with so many just to buy a lad a drink. After the game they came back into town looking for another go but we missed them. They left messages in a couple of bars saying they were going to do this and that to Paul Durrant. A few years later I was abroad watching England and I was being interviewed on television. A few of the lads around me heard me say I was from Bradford. Afterwards they came up to me and started talking about Paul Durrant. They'd not forgotten the kicking they got in Bradford. I got pissed off with them eventually and cleared off from the moaning.

Cardiff Soul Crew
Cardiff City (A)
27/11/93

Steff

WE took a double decker coach down full of lads that would have taken an awful lot of shifting. Having said that you are apprehensive about what's in front of you. They had a big reputation and we weren't taking big numbers down. We got to Cardiff just after opening time and headed for the Soul Crew's boozer. Some of their lads were inside when we arrived. One was a lippy cunt and he got punched in the face. Cardiff say we were out of order smacking this lad. But he shot his mouth off and paid for it. Besides, this was no game, we were here to do Cardiff. They all left with the lippy lad shouting they would be back with all their boys. Even the landlord was warning us the Soul Crew would arrive. We fully expected a load to turn up anytime but they didn't. We ended up walking about Cardiff looking for them. The old bill eventually wrapped us up and walked us to Ninian Park. Inside the ground we were in the seats at the side and you could see Cardiff had a good mob out. During the match two Soul Crew lads were in the away toilets. One was supposed to have been their hard man. He knew the name of a very handy Bradford lad and wanted a one-on-one. It's alright saying that with scores of old bill about. The Cardiff fella is lucky his wish wasn't granted. He got squirted in the face with tomato ketchup though.

After the game the police tried to keep us in so we ended up kicking a door down to get out. Cardiff appeared across the car park outside the stadium and there were loads of them. There was a bit of running backwards and forwards. They kept stopping and egging us to go into this estate. But it had ambush written all over it. There could have been hundreds of the cunts in there. So we just stayed where we were. It was on them to come at us. We left disappointed with Cardiff. It was pretty much a non-event.

Cardiff City (H)
07/05/94

Chris

IN the return fixture Cardiff brought about 200 up and fair play for bringing the numbers. They had a few Leeds lads with them who knew Annis Abraham and they were taking them around. Some of the Service Crew lads hate Bradford with a passion and if they knew lads in other firms they often tag along showing them the Ointment pubs and stuff. But as for Cardiff, they had old bill all over them. There were pockets of stuff going off and one of ours fired a distress flare into them near the Kirkgate Centre. They also tried to storm a boozer called the Market Tavern where about thirty Ointment were in. But they got no further than the door and a Cardiff lad at the front got dragged into the bar and got a good kicking. So everything was sporadic and in little bursts. Cardiff claim they had us before the game but if you call running about with loads of police a result then fair enough. But after the game there was no doubt who came out on top. Word had got round that Cardiff had brought a good team over and we had got our act together with loads milling about outside waiting for the game to finish. There must have been a good 200 + waiting for the Soul Crew outside Valley Parade. As soon as the game was over we went round the back of the away end as Cardiff came out. It's a very narrow street where the away end was in those days, the old Bradford End. As they came out we came around the corner and the street was just full of lads fighting. The police had lost it as they had one mob coming up the street and another coming down it. Cardiff stood toe-to-toe with us for about a minute and they had a good few who were game. But as more and more Ointment came down the hill Cardiff either backed off or went back into the ground. More and more police arrived and they were chasing us chasing Cardiff down towards the Midland Road. Those that ran back in the ground only came back out when the filth swamped the place. Whatever gains Cardiff thought they had made before the game were quickly wiped out after. I've spoken to the Service Crew lads who were with Cardiff that day and even they admit we had them after the game. You cannot knock them for bringing a very decent mob up. They also came into Bradford looking for it. But like many others in the past they underestimated what they would come up against. Cardiff had done a little show around town but after the game we had lads out to give them what they came looking for.

Leicester City Baby Squad
Play-Off's (In London)
27/05/ 96

Crowy
WE had loads out for Notts County but we split up with a coach breaking down and traffic and vans getting lost and stuff. Altogether City had over 31,000 at Wembley for this Sunday game. Two van loads of us had arrived in London and we were near The Globe Pub in Marylebone. Twenty of us walked up and there was a decent firm of about 60 outside that turned out to be Leicester Baby Squad. They were playing in the play-offs on the Bank Holiday Monday. We were embarrassed really as there was so few of us. They started giving it all the bollox about having 300 lads dotted about and taking the piss out of us. Had it been the other

way round we might have done the same but we were not backing down. But you could tell they were up for doing us. This big lad with an adidas cagoule had the biggest mouth out of all of them. He said: "Ointment? Is this all you have? Right seeing as you have shit numbers I'll fight any one of you one-on-one around the back. Hardest one, round the back."

So quick as a flash Dean took his teeth out and said: "Come on then, I'll fight you."

The big silly bastard put his drink down but forgot who agreed to fight him and told me to come round the corner. Eventually him and Dean both set off down the street to have a do. The Baby Squad lads were saying Dean would get hammered and to be honest he was a big fella this Leicester lad. But all of a sudden this tosser turns round and heads back to The Globe.

"I've had a load of E's, I'm off my head and don't feel well," he says.

The Baby Squad were fucking red-faced, shaking their heads in embarrassment. Later Dean told us he thought he was going to get murdered, but as they went down the road the Leicester lad told him he'd changed his mind. We stayed for a drink and you could sense it might kick-off at anytime. The guy who bottled it still could not remember who had agreed to fight him and was saying to me : "Fair play for walking down the street with me. I'm sorry I don't know what I'm doing."

Another funny thing about it was when we started to walk away from the pub, this same silly cunt shouts: "We've 300 at Covent Garden."

We've taken the piss at Leicester every time we've played them at Filbert Street. If our mob had bumped into them over that weekend we would have given them it. A few years later they brought 100 lads to Bradford when we

85

were in the Premier League. They scattered a few of ours near the Train Station and a little fat twat pulled a blade out on me. But that's the only time Leicester can claim any sort of result against us. The Baby Squad gained a good reputation during the 80's because they were mixing it with the top mobs in the country. If they are a marker, then the Ointment would have done very well.

Leicester (A)
01/01/01

Mark

THREE coaches of us went down on New Year's Day. By this time we knew we were getting relegated so everyone was making the best of it. Most of us were pissed before the coaches even left Bradford. We'd been to Leicester before in the late 80's and taken the piss. We are down around Filbert Street having a drink, wandering about and stuff but found nothing. We got rounded up outside the ground and the police had us all lined up against the back of one of the stands. The line went as far as you could see, it seemed like it had gone from one end to the other. The Inspector in charge was shitting his pants, shouting out orders to find this lot's coaches and stuff. They put us back on the buses and escorted us for 50 miles up the M1. We didn't even get the chance to see the game.

Chapter Eleven
LONG DISTANCE RIVAL

IN the late 70's and early 80's games with Portsmouth were the highlight of the Bradford hooligan calendar. Both teams had a good away following and the long trip left many fuelled up for a fight on arrival. In 1979, over 22,000 watched a Division Four clash between the two sides at Fratton Park. The 6.57 crew turned out both home & away. They were the only club who had the numbers to rival the Ointment in the basement division during this period. Clashes between the two mobs often led to scores of arrests.

Portsmouth (A)
02/01/78

General
THIS was a match where the old Town Boys and the newly formed and mainly younger Ointment travelled separately. The Town Boys took a coach from Scamps Night Club in the early hours and us lot set off at eight in the morning. Portsmouth had a reputation at the time of chasing away fans onto the pitch from the open end behind the goal. It was a small terrace that pretty much had no segregation. So we were aware that it was likely to kick-off. We got into the ground and headed to the front of the terrace. We were all young at the time and thought we could have it with anyone.

But after a while small groups of these ugly big Portsmouth bastards started hanging around us. More and more kept on coming and you could feel it was going to start soon. I remember a ditch that ran in front of the terrace and I said to myself: "I'm going to end up in that head first." But then I noticed one of the Town Boys walk past, then another, then another. A lad called Geffro, who was into Martial Arts, whispered in my ear: "We're going to steam this lot in a minute, any of you lot run and we'll kick your fucking heads in later." He then walked on. There were some black lads in the Town Boys and I remember a few had these long Afghan coats on. They looked like pimps. In a second it went off and the Town Boys were getting stuck into Portsmouth from the side and behind. I'm not sure if they had seen many black lads fighting at football before but they ran back up the terrace and some got battered in the turnstiles trying to get out. For us it was fucking great to see as we thought we were about to get hammered. One Portsmouth lad was lying on the floor and someone said: "He's got a Seiko watch on." They were well smart in those days and he got that robbed off him. As this is going off loads of Portsmouth are trying to get over from the side. There was only a small gate and they were only getting through in dribs and drabs. A copper eventually shut the gate and it was a good job as hundreds of Pompey were trying to get to us. After the game we were escorted back to the coaches and every fucking window was put through on three coaches. We got to Oxford and coaches with windows were waiting to take us back home. But the trip up there was good as we seemed to stop in every other town for a drink to get warm.

Portsmouth (A)
19/08/78

General

TWO coach loads of us got to Portsmouth early morning again. There was nothing open so some of us went over to the Isle of Wight. When we got there we found an off-licence and we were having a kick about on the beach when loads of old bill arrived. Someone asked why they were hassling us when we had done nothing wrong. A sergeant pointed out to sea and said: "It's not you lads, it's those out there." Peter Newby and three others had swum out to this yacht and were drinking its booze cabinet empty while sunbathing on deck. The police brought them back to port and put us all back on the ferry to the mainland. It was full of Portsmouth but they didn't give us any grief. This time at the ground we were given the whole end to ourselves behind the goal. Portsmouth were trying to storm the gates at the side to get in at us. After the game loads of them were trying to get at us near the back of the ground and the police had put a line of vans between us. The Portsmouth lads were surging forwards and rocking them. There were hundreds of them up this narrow road. If the vans and the coppers had not been there I'd say we might have been in trouble.

Portsmouth (A)
20/10/79

Steff

SIX hundred went down on a football special and the vast majority onboard were up for a row. It started a stop before Portsmouth when some of their lads on the station platform and on a grass bank started stoning the train. Someone pulled the emergency cord and we got off and ran back up the tracks towards the cunts. They fucked off quickly. Some of the lads never got back on the train and made their own way to Fratton Park. The old bill came on the train with us to Portsmouth. When we arrived loads of Pompey were waiting on the streets outside for us. We got escorted up to the ground and we started to pay into the ground. There was so many of us trying to get in everyone was pushing. Not enough gates were open and it was chaos. After a couple of minutes they shut the turnstiles as the old bill tried to sort everything out. But 40 City fans had already been let in and left like lambs to the slaughter. Pompey lads came over the terracing and pitch at these poor cunts and fucking hammered them. You could see through the gaps in the turnstiles the City lot getting a kicking. You could hear it too. One lad tried to get out and was left wrapped around a turnstile. The old bill were letting it happen. We were going mental outside as the dog handlers tried to keep us from storming the ground. During the match there were scuffles on the side of the pitch and stuff but no one seemed to get nicked in the ground. They were just throwing people out. After the game there were running battles all the way to the train station and this time loads were getting lifted.

Portsmouth (H)
01/03/80

General
POMPEY brought four thousand fans up for this game. They had loads of skinheads with them and most had come by a special train. At the time a load of terrace houses around Valley Parade were being demolished and there was bricks and debris lying about everywhere. Portsmouth completely filled one half of the Kop which was a very rare sight in those days as most clubs would only bring a few

hundred away supporters or less. What used to happen was that City fans would pick up bricks from the demolition site and throw them over the wall into the away section of the Kop. I remember looking up and the blue sky was being crossed by a hail of bricks cascading onto the Pompey supporters. They were firing them back into the City fans on the other side too. During the game both sets of fans made attempts to scale the fences separating them but were beaten back by the police. Portsmouth lads did manage to get on the pitch and there was a bit of fighting at full-time but nothing major. After the game thousands of Pompey fans were escorted the mile or so back into town for the train back home. We attacked it a few times and Portsmouth would also make attempts to break the escort. Unfortunately I got nicked along with dozens more. The cells in the police station were jammed with lads from both sides. I got out about 10 pm and as I was at the charge desk I spotted a lad called Tommo being frogmarched in for fighting Pompey lads. I was surprised that it was still going off so late into the night. It turned out some Ointment were waiting near the police station for Portsmouth lads who had been arrested to be let out and then give them a kicking. Tommo had chased one back into the station and thrown him through a glass window. When he went to court the judge asked him what possessed him to attack a Portsmouth fan in a police station. He replied: "Because he thought he was safe."

Steff
EVERYONE was out for this game and we were in the Royal Standard waiting. A couple of hours before kick-off one of the lads came in and said 40 Portsmouth were in the Bradford Arms. We went over and sure enough all these skinheads were in watching horse racing. They all had Donkey Jackets on. To be honest they had no chance as they

were well outnumbered. Ointment lads were coming in through the front and side doors and getting stuck in. Fists, boots and everything not bolted down were raining down on these poor cunts. This Pompey lad launched a television with the horse racing on through the window and they all started to escape out of the gap. But they were jumping into loads of our lot outside and they got fucking battered. There were a couple of funny things about this incident. Firstly, the old bill came and nicked the Pompey lads who got battered and left us alone. Secondly, the television that came through the window was plugged in and the horse racing was still on.

Traci Dadd, Coatsey, Andy Larkin, Eddie and Tony Cuss.

Chapter Twelve
LUNATICS IN THE ASYLUM

Derby County
10/11/84

THIS was the first time City had played Derby in 30 years. It was also another opportunity for the Ointment to give a highly regarded firm a hiding. Tensions had been building up prior to this match as former manager Roy McFarland had walked out on City two years previously in controversial circumstances after being 'poached' by Derby. Walking out on a club was pretty rare in this era and the incident made all the back pages at the time. The Rams were eventually fined £10,000 and ordered to pay £55,000 compensation. So there was bad blood between the two clubs despite the long gap not playing one another. McFarland himself needed a police escort to and from the dugout for his own protection. County's thugs were known as the Derby Lunatic Fringe (DLF). They had established a good reputation in the top divisions over the years so it was expected they would show. And they did, before the game in town, and in Bradford's seats at the start of the game. What many of the Ointment remember is a few of the DLF were black lads wearing camouflage type clothing.

One of them was a Rasta. Paul Durrant who is an ex-soldier got talking to a few Derby lads that day and they were still serving in the Royal Anglian Regiment. Thirty six arrests were made at the game which was the highest number since 64 got lifted during the Sheffield United match three years earlier.

Telegraph & Argus report:
"Rival fans hurled missiles, including lumps of concrete at the open end of the ground and there was fighting in the stand, seats were uprooted and thrown down onto the terraces."

In a frank admission the City chairman at the time, Stafford Heginbotham, admitted trouble had been expected on the Kop, where rival supporters were separated by two metal fences and a no-man's land area. He said the club had flooded the area with policemen.

However, it was not enough, as mass disorder erupted both on the Kop and in the main stand. The terracing at Bradford at the time was falling to bits and if you kicked it, bits would crumble off. And on many occasions the concrete was used to throw at away fans on the other side of the fence. Lower league supporters were used to getting pelted at Valley Parade and many never came back. But for the bigger clubs, who Bradford were now playing for the first time, it was a shock.

Scores of Derby and City fans received attention from the St John's Ambulance for head and facial wounds after being struck by flying objects. Many were taken down the no-man's area in the Kop with blood spilling down their faces. This type of hooliganism is indiscriminate and many innocent supporters were injured. In the seats however the Ointment was at it with the DLF and the fighting was being broadcast live to listeners in Derbyshire. The commentator described it as one of the scariest moments of his life.

Chris

I WAS in the Kop and I saw the trouble in the seats. Everyone was up for it because of the McFarland thing. In those days in the old Kop there was a small gap in the fence to get onto the pitch. I noticed the old bill were queuing up to get to all the bother that was going on in the stand. The game had stopped at this time and the violence was mentioned on the Saturday afternoon sports show Grandstand. I got in the paddock, a standing area in front of the stand, and could see dozens of one-to-one scraps going off in the seats. As I was pulling myself up to where all the fighting was, a black DLF kid gave me a right boot in the face and nearly took my head off. I managed to get in the seats though. The police were weighing in with truncheons while others shit it and ran off to the back of the stand. More and more Ointment were turning up in the Paddock and climbing over into the seats to join the fun. The DLF by now had realised they made a mistake thinking they could take the piss. They thought they were the misters coming in our seats. But not for long. Fair play to Derby for having a go but they got swamped. After about five minutes of non-stop fighting we did the cunts. Some were left bloodied and slumped over seats while the others kicked a door down at the back of the stand to get out. In the Kop they were getting pelted with stuff all through the game. You almost felt sorry for Derby that day, they were really getting hammered. Unlike many others though, they had a go and came looking for it. The DLF were in town early doors and dotted themselves about the ground. Respect where it's due. A lot of the Ointment have time for Derby after that show.

Jimmy

ALL the lads met in The Queen and were expecting Derby to be early arrivals so the place was packed with lads.

However, they never showed and everyone made their way from pub to pub towards Valley Parade. A bad fault of Bradford's at that time, and even now, was that everyone would split up and just head for next pub because they couldn't be arsed waiting. We were made to pay for it this time at the top end of town. The small group I was with were heading for the Theatre Tavern when a shout went up behind us. We turned and headed back towards The Star pub but it was chaos with people running in all directions. Derby had arrived. Across the street was a supermarket and tins of beans and stuff were flying towards the Derby lads. One of our lads rammed into the lot of them with a shopping trolley. Now to be completely honest I wasn't too keen heading up to The Star as there were only a handful of us.

A lad called Torchy went passed me towards all the commotion. I feel bad about this as a while later I saw he was covered in blood and had been given a hiding by Derby. To this day I hate myself for not going up the road with him. But later I got a bit of personal redemption. Inside the ground was mental. We were all in our usual spot off the left corner of the stand and paddock. But Derby managed to pay in the main stand too and they had the top left corner. I remember two big black lads wearing army gear sat in the middle of our lot. I'd say there was about 40 DLF in the main stand. There was an uneasy atmosphere with the old bill swarming all over the seats. But as soon as the first goal went in the place erupted. Chunks of concrete were being thrown from the crumbling terraces and fences were being ripped down as fans went for one another. Those two lads in army gear soon shifted and vanished. I remember an old head called Housey hitting them with his crutches. But to be fair to Derby, they were well up for it but had to back off or they would have been seriously hurt. The police had run for cover too. I got smashed in the face with a seat by one of our

96

own lads called Ginner! The old bill made 36 arrests in the ground that day.

Gavin, (DLF)
"That day at Bradford was a proper full on day. Our lot went by early train and knew there would be trouble following the Roy McFarland managerial saga. There was still a lot of bad feeling amongst the clubs. It started early doors for us, changing trains at Leeds and clashing with a load of Service Crew at Leeds station, then on arriving at Bradford, the theme continued all day. During the game inside Valley Parade was mental at times ...fair play to Bradford, a very eventful day."

Chapter Thirteen

OVER THE HILL

THE red rose county of Lancashire is a hotbed of football hooligan firms. Many of these lads are associated with unglamorous small town clubs. But that doesn't mean they couldn't put a decent mob out. On occasions these Lancashire sides could muster firms of 100 plus.

Some also had the sharpest dressers anywhere during the casual scene. The likes of Wigan were just as smart as the Liverpool or Manchester hooligans who led the way in the fashion stakes. The mill town clubs had tight-knit gangs that took some shifting. The Bradford Ointment had many rows with lads from across the Pennines going back to the 70's. From pitch invasions, dawn raids and wrecking stands. There is a history of 'trouble at t'mill' with these tough hooligan gangs.

Stockport County (A)
19/10/81

Chris
A VAN full of us parked away from the ground as the year before our transport had been turned over. It was the time you went in the away ends. We got in about 15 minutes into the match and City was losing 2-0. A couple of us paid into the Stockport end and waited for the Ointment to

arrive. We'd had so many fights with Stockport that they knew who Andy Naylor was and when City arrived in their end it kicked off straight away. Me and my mate were at the opposite side and had to push our way through hordes of Stockport to get to the Ointment lads. A big circle had formed around the Ointment. This was proper fighting, none of the hand bag stuff. The coppers who had been there had left with the City lads they arrested. We were hitting Stockport lads as we were making our way through and they had no idea what was going on. But just as I got in with the Ointment, some fella spun me around and smashed me in the face, breaking my nose. As the fighting went on uninterrupted City scored two goals to make the Stockport lads even more up for it. The whole end was having a pop. Eventually the police split us up and walked us around the ground where the away support was. All the City fans were singing:

"We're proud of you."

I felt like ten men, only my face was splattered with my nose pointing the wrong way so that took the shine off it a bit. When we got put back in with the City fans a copper said he thought my nose was broke and he grabbed it and pulled it back into shape.

Bizarrely a note in the Stockport programme asked for Andy Naylor and his friends from Bradford to behave.

Wigan (H)
19/11/83

Jimmy

WIGAN took us by surprise at this one. I don't remember anything occurring before the game or even noticing their lads during match to be honest, so I don't think we expected anything from Wigan. It was in the FA Cup and the game finished 0-0. A few of us were heading back into town and we were just passing what used to be Caesars Nightclub when 60 Wigan charged us from a side street. They took us all by surprise and our lads were split all over the place so it was up to the 20 or so that were there to hold ground. Luckily for us a few scarfers backed us and we got Wigan to back off a bit. A building brick came flying past my head and straight into my mate's face, who was sparked straight away. There was one Wigan lad with a green Fila BJ, who was fucking well game. He was knocking a few over then disappearing back into their mob before coming out again and repeating the trick. To be honest Wigan were getting the upper hand until a few more of our lads got to us. We managed to back them to the opposite side of Manningham Lane where there was a bit of a stand-off. Wigan surged forward again, with the lad in the Fila BJ at the front and it was toe-to-toe until the coppers arrived. I give credit to Wigan for bringing it to us that day.

Wigan (H)
27/12/83

WE expected Wigan to turn up this time and The Queen was packed with lads. Word came that Wigan had a few up near the ground already and some more had just got off the train at Forster Square. We split up and went looking for them in both places but Wigan were nowhere to be seen. After the game everyone headed for Forster Square and we came across about 50 of the cunts. They were shit this time and scattered but then a mini-bus full of them appeared and drove straight towards a good mob of ours coming down Manor Row. The driver did the quickest three-point turn in history and headed back down towards us. They were fucked. As the van stopped with nowhere to go everyone started rocking it. The old bill came just before this mini-bus went over.

Bolton (A)
06/05/85

Chris

OVER 5,000 City fans were at this game including a good 300 lads. This was the first time the younger lot, Section Five, made an appearance, in numbers too. Two coaches of the usual lot went early while the rest, plus Section Five, got the service train to Bolton. This turned out to be a great day for violence both inside and outside the ground. Those on the coaches got to a pub not far from the old Burnden Park ground at opening time and we were not there long before it kicked-off. About 20 of us were drinking outside when 100 odd Bolton came charging around the corner. They caught us a bit by surprise having that many out so early in the morning. But as some of ours tried to get Bradford out the landlord bolted the door. We were fucked. The only thing we could do was hold the line until the rest managed to get out of the pub. We clashed in the middle of the road and we were backing off at first as Bolton overpowered us. But as more and more Ointment came out of the back of the pub things started to even themselves out. It was proper toe-to-toe. It was a real brawl for a few minutes with skirmishes going on in the road and in the pub car park. As the police started to arrive Bolton fucked off but not before one of theirs fired a flare into the middle of us all. The coppers were cunts here and were nicking people at random. The rest of us were marched into the ground early. We were put in some seats at the side while most fans were behind the goal. As kick-off approached plastic seats began to be ripped up by both sets of fans and thrown at one another along with hot drinks. About 10 minutes into the match those who had come on the service train arrived and it was not long before fighting broke out in the standing area on the opposite side of the ground. Fair play to Bolton for having a right go. They even kicked down the turnstile doors in the stand we were in and came in for a do at half-time. Loads of people were being taken onto the side of the pitch with injuries and bloodied heads. Bolton fans were also pelting our players with coins and meat pies. In one newspaper it reported Bradford fans had smashed a stand up but Bolton would not be taking it further as they were taking the seats out anyway in pre-season!

Oldham (A)
01/04/89

Badger
ABOUT 60 of us left early in vans and stopped off in Rochdale and had a row with some of their lads. I got a brick smashed into my face so by the time we got to Oldham I had this huge shiner. Before the game there was about a 100 Ointment in Oldham town centre. They got their act together and must have realised we had a decent firm as they piled out of bars and started pelting us with beer glasses from all directions. Their main mob, known as the Fine Young Casuals (FYC), was in a pub up some steps. We charged that and apart from a few they all ran back inside and bolted the doors behind them. We just walked through the flying beer glasses and annihilated them. One game Oldham lad got his ear bitten off. Funny thing about that was a season later he was hanging about outside the away turnstiles asking people if they knew who had bitten his ear off! We paid into the Oldham seats but nothing happened during the game. But after the match six of us got

left in Oldham when our van driver left us behind. We made our way to the train station when my mate came running up a field shouting: "They are here."

I looked down towards this subway and walking towards us at pace were about 40 Oldham lads tooled up. They had bats, sticks, steel poles, the lot. As they got closer we had to get on our toes. We got to this fence and they were right behind us. As I got over I turned around and smacked one Oldham lad off the fence and then another before we all made our way over this field. We noticed they were no longer behind us and the adrenalin rush caused us all to start laughing uncontrollably. It must have been the relief as well.

But as we got to the end of the field a line of cars came screeching up the road. It was the Oldham FYC again. We were in this real Asian area of town by now. One of our lads was a Sikh who could speak their lingo and he was talking to them. We piled into this corner shop as the Oldham lads pulled over in their cars. Within seconds all the windows of the shop went through and this set off the local Muslims. They came running out of their houses and were having it with the Oldham lads who were after our blood. Even little kids were throwing bricks at them. I've no doubt these Asians saved our arses.

Burnley & Stockport (A)
26/01/90

Crowy

A FEW of our lads knew some Stockport who they had met on holiday. They were playing Burnley away and asked if we wanted to meet them. So a few of us decided to go over in a van for the laugh. We were having a pint in this boozer and a few Burnley Suicide Squad came in. One asked us if we were Stockport and before any of us could say anything he started taking the piss saying County had only brought 12 lads. I told him we were Bradford and he could not understand it. He wanted to know what we were doing and I told him we had come to do Burnley and Stockport. So he's like:

"You what? We have 100 lads up at Yates's."

"Come up and have a pint with us you daft cunts. "

I replied: "Are you deaf? We've come to do you and Stockport."

We were taking the piss out of him and this daft cunt fuck's off. We knew it wouldn't be long before Burnley showed up so we went up to Yates's ourselves. It was a lovely sunny day and right enough we spotted a load of Burnley outside Yates's. It was a paved pedestrian area and loads of shoppers were out. They saw us and came steaming into us. We knocked a few heads but there was just too many and they were giving us a good kicking. The old bill arrived and Burnley went back to the pub. It sounds daft with the police about but we were pissed off we had just got a hiding so we steamed back into a few of them at the pub. They came running out again and gave us another hiding. I remember lying on the floor in a load of broken glass as feet are competing to kick me in the head.

Wigan (H)
27/10/90

Paul Durrant
THIS is an incident that still causes arguments in Bradford today. I was in the bookies on Manningham Lane when a lad comes running in saying Wigan are here. I walked out and there is about 60 Wigan outside the Bradford Arms goading people inside. Myself, Affon, and a lad called Cough ran towards them thinking we were going to get

smashed. As we got closer they started to panic and a few started to run, then a few more, until eventually the lot of them were off. We couldn't understand it. We got to the Bradford Arms and we realised some of our lot were inside. It turned out that Wigan had chased some of our lads into the pub and when they got in one of them locked the door. No one has ever owned up to it. But for a few minutes City lads were trapped inside while Wigan laid siege to the place. The only explanation as to why Wigan ran off is that they must have thought we had started to come out of another door in the pub. If they hadn't have ran off they would have realised there was only three of us and we would have been in big trouble.

Burnley (H)
29/01/91

Francis
THIS was a Leyland Daf Cup game and no one was taking it seriously. It was a night match and only about 10 of us were out. We went to the Belle Vue near the ground for a pint. What we didn't know was Burnley had brought a mob over and they were inside. We went to the bar and were immediately surrounded by the Suicide Squad. There were around 50 of them, pissed, and looking for a row. Two of our lads went to the toilet and were followed and took a bit of a kicking. The rest started on us. My mate Cody had never left a pint in his life but we ran out of the pub with Burnley behind smacking us with fists and pool cues. Thankfully they didn't bother chasing us too far as Crowy had taken a kick in the balls. It was a shock they had brought any lads never mind 50. It was before mobile phones so we went to a phone box ringing houses to try and get some lads down. Just before kick-off we managed to get

about 20 together and had it with them outside the ground. We were still well outnumbered and getting done. Then Dean Brimacombe came from nowhere and steamed into a big group of them. They started to panic and surprisingly scattered. Burnley legged it and we went after them. At the game we were surprised how many fans they had brought, nearly 3,000. They were treating it like an important FA cup tie or something. After the match 50 of us had gathered but nothing happened.

Stockport County (A)
05/10/91

Steff
SIX weeks before this game we played at Stockport in the Rumbelows Cup. A coach of us went over and ran them ragged in the town centre and took over their pub. We went over again for this match in a coach and vans and the plan was to have a drink. When we arrived they had a welcoming committee waiting and it went off. Again Stockport got done big time. The small shopping precinct was left like a war zone with windows broken and littered with debris and bins. The whole thing however had been captured on police cameras. Six months later dawn raids were carried out in Bradford and Greater Manchester. Eventually six members of the Ointment were jailed.

Telegraph & Argus:
"Eleven men were arrested and a cache of weapons were seized in a swoop on football hooligans. Police raided houses in the Buttershaw, Holmewood, West Bowling and Fagley areas of Bradford at 6 am. At the same time arrests were made in the Stockport area. The raids were aimed at arresting ringleaders of the two gangs of soccer thugs - the

Ointment gang from Bradford and the Stockport Mafia. One suspected hooligan put up a violent struggle at a house in Fagley. Police had to call for back-up and the man was eventually subdued. Weapons were later found at one of the houses in Bradford and taken to Manchester for examination."

Chester City (A)
13/08/94

Paul Durrant

WE had over 100 lads out for this game as it was sunny and we were heading to Blackpool afterwards. There were numerous pitch invasions and at least half the crowd were from Bradford. There was no one to have a do with so our lot turned on the police and were pelting them with bricks outside the ground at the end of the game. I was pissed off as I was the only person to get hit by one and I had blood streaming down my face. We ended up in Blackpool and headed for the popular Manchester Bar. As I'm going in one of the doormen told me I couldn't come in as my head was still bleeding but he would go get me a bandage. So I patched my head up and everyone is having a laugh. There were always a lot of drugs about on these trips although I did not touch them myself. The bar was a magnet for Hen and Stag Nights at the time and there were groups from all over the place. After a few hours it kicked off with our lot and the bouncers. What sticks in my mind was the bouncer who had helped patch up my head wound was being used in a tug-of-war by four Ointment lads. He was in a star shape as they stretched him. I felt very bad about this as he'd helped me.

Preston North End (H)
02/12/95

Chris

THERE were a handful of us hanging about the Midland Road waiting for any stragglers after the game. Then out of the thick fog loads of Preston were charging towards us. We were on our toes and you could hear the bastards right behind us. But thankfully they stopped. I suspect they did not want to go too far into the unknown as you could not see a few yards in front of you because of the fog. We got into town and we were boiling about it to be honest. I fucking hate being run. A few more of ours had got together now and we heard Preston had come by train. It wasn't long before they came marching through with a small police escort. They had a good 40 lads and we steamed straight into them. This big fucker with them clocked for me and said:

"You might do us, but I'm going to knock your fucking head in."

Trust me to land a cunt like this. Anyway he never did anything and I cracked him. But fair play to Preston. This will never go down as the biggest battle in football history, but it was a right do. Proper full on. Neither set of lads gave an inch until the old bill laid into us all with truncheons. For some reason they didn't seem interested in arresting anyone.

Burnley (H)
28/10/95

Francis

LOADS of lads were on banning orders and getting jail during this period. Many were not bothering with football.

Burnley had turned up years before in a Leyland Daf match but had done nothing else of note. When we went over they were never about either. So in hindsight most had taken this match too lightly. I was in town with Steff having a pint and we were talking about going to the casino. We weren't thinking about the match at all. A lad had mentioned to us he had seen a load of Burnley but we just dismissed it. We were heading up towards the casino when we noticed some lads outside St George's Hall opposite. We went over and it turned out it was Burnley. We had no idea how many were inside. A few words were said and one of the Burnley lads said they were celebrating a birthday and they didn't want any hassle. Fair enough, so we fucked off to the casino. A few hours later we went to The Queen. At the bar I could feel a sort of tension and when I looked to my right I knew why. There must have been 100 Burnley packed in the top of the bar. All lads. Steff said: "I'm off to the toilet." And I said:

"Fuck this I'm coming with you."

We had a chat and a piss then walked back out. As soon as we left the toilet they came at us, shouting and screaming. I jumped over a table and legged it out of the door and Steff ran behind the bar. I ran down the street and into a phone box. I rang one of the lads and they were in Wibsey playing cards. I told them to come down but no one was bothered.

Preston North End (A)
26/04/03

Francis

MORE than 100 of us went over for this game and we got nothing before the match. The game was crap so about 25 of us left early and went for a pint in Preston. One of our lads went for a wander and came back saying some Preston were in a pub down the road. A few went down but most stayed where we were as you could see the CCTV cameras watching our every move. There was a small scale battle that ended up on YouTube but nothing major. The Preston lads had a go and didn't budge. Only two police were on the scene at the beginning. They were grabbing people and then telling them to stay before going after someone else. Nobody stayed where they were. More police arrived and we got escorted to the train station and met more of our lads.

We got on the train and got off again at Blackburn. What a dead end place that is. We pretty much took the town centre over. They had a few about but they were like rabbits in headlights. While we were there one of our lads got a call from a Service Crew lad saying they had 200 waiting for us in pubs near Leeds train station. The line from Blackburn went straight to Bradford and we'd done enough running around for one day.

Chapter Fourteen

DOWN TOWN

ONE mob the Ointment has crossed paths with many times over the years has been the Huddersfield Young Casuals (HYC). The fortunes of both clubs over the last four decades have been pretty similar. They have met regularly in three divisions of the football league and understandably a keen local rivalry developed both on and off the pitch. But with a population less than half of Bradford's, and a much smaller pool of lads to call upon, many Ointment members dismiss Town as serious football hooligan rivals. They feel when it comes down to it, Huddersfield just can't compete with big city rivals.

Some also argue that many of the rows in the past have been with members of the West Indian community in the Fartown area of Huddersfield rather than the HYC. However, clashes involving the two groups have led to extreme violence, long prison sentences, stabbings and the tragic death of a young Bradford fan. The HYC has turned out at home, and on occasions made an effort away. It has gained a reputation for punching above its weight. So called 'bigger' teams have come unstuck in Huddersfield after taking them lightly. What follows is a selection of violent confrontations seen through the eyes of some of the Ointments most well know lads.

Paul Whitehead

Huddersfield (A)
01/01/83
TWO coaches went to Huddersfield early doors and the plan was to all go in the big home end at the side of the pitch. Everything was closed and we were wandering around the town centre trying to find a pub open. Eventually the owner of a West Indian club opened up to let us all in. The fella was delighted with this unexpected business and before long he had a couple of strippers doing their stuff to keep us entertained. We stayed in there a couple of hours and got no trouble. As we walked up to the ground we approached two pubs that were supposed to be full of their lads. One was called the Market Tavern. We steamed the first bar and some of our lads managed to get inside. During a scuffle one Huddersfield lad got stabbed. No one ever got done for it. The police came and we headed for the ground. By this time we had split up or got wrapped up by the police. So only 20 of us managed to get into the Huddersfield side of the ground. The game itself was a disaster for City and we eventually lost 6-3. We had a defender at the time Cess Podd, who still holds the record for appearances at Bradford City. He played 565 times for the club but only scored three goals in all that time, one was in this game. All 20 of us went mad when he scored and we fully expected Huddersfield to have a go. But despite being well outnumbered they did not come at us so we steamed into them. Bad mistake. Suddenly they all came flying into us. We were fucked. We were trapped in the corner as wave after wave of Town fans came at us. It seemed like the whole end was up for it. We were forced to the front as City fans attempted to scale the fences in the away end to come and help us. After a few minutes the police managed to put

a line around us to save our arses. They took us out through a gate and as we looked to our left a big mob of City were waiting to pay in the Huddersfield end. Some of them started cheering when they saw us and the old bill sussed who they were and took us all round to the away end. If that mob had got into the home end, Town would have been well and truly fucked. The old bill in those days would just take you out and put you in the right end of the ground, whereas now you'd be nicked.

Jimmy

Huddersfield (H)
14/05/83
TOWN had come to celebrate promotion and they brought 4,000 supporters over. We used to meet in city centre bar The Unicorn in those days. Around mid-day word came they had a mob two miles away in the Lister's Arms on Manchester Road. We split up into two groups to stretch the old bill. The older heads went off the main road and came in at the Lister's near St. Joseph's Church, while the Junior Ointment marched direct up Manchester Road.

Huddersfield were in the car-park at the front and would see the younger lads coming. Indeed they were concentrating on what was coming up the road when the main City mob attacked them from behind. The few who were drinking in the car-park shot back inside the pub and bolted the door behind them. Then all hell broke loose. All the windows in the bar were put through with the Town lads throwing stools and tables back out of the pub. Our lot managed to get the door open and fighting went off in the doorway. Punches were being thrown through the broken windows as over 100 Ointment laid siege to the pub. This went on for a good 10 minutes before the police arrived.

We all ran off and Huddersfield, who seemed to be all skinheads, came after us before thinking better of it. Back in the city-centre the younger lads went to the Boy & Barrel and having a good laugh about what had happened. Then one lad ran in and shouted Town were coming up Ivegate. We charged down and straight into them. The group I was with chased a few into a clothes shop called the Wagon Wheel. These lads got fucking battered in his shop. I remember the till was wide open with notes begging to be taken, but in all the frenzy nobody thought to nick it. By this time more Huddersfield and more of us were clashing in different places all over town. We came across some more on Manor Row and once again it went off with lads from both sides getting put on their arses. In the ground Huddersfield were given both sides of the Kop which meant we all went into the stand/paddock area at the side. It wasn't long before trouble started with bricks, bottles, and concrete flying from both sides. Funny thing with the Kop was at the bottom right corner was a pie stand which had hatches to feed both the Kop side and the paddock, so you could actually jump through the hatch if you were stupid enough. Well fuck me, fighting broke out in the bottom corner and all of a sudden I saw this lad with a blue and white scarf jump through the pie stand and land right in the middle of us lot in the paddock. That bloke alone got my vote of the day as he was a lunatic. We won the game 3-1, and after, pockets of trouble broke out around the ground. All in all I've got to give respect to Huddersfield this time as they did come and they brought a fight. They even had a go at taking our main boozer in town at the time, The Unicorn.

Telegraph and Argus report:
"Rival soccer fans went on the rampage as the football season ended in violence. Ugly scenes of vandalism brought

terror to the city before and after Saturday's match between Bradford City and Huddersfield Town. In one incident, rival supporters hurled bricks and stools through windows at the Lister's Arms pub in Manchester Road. Landlord Albert Chappell branded the vandalism as "soccer madness". Around 60 arrests were made before and after the Third Division clash. Mr Chappell said: "What I saw here made me quite sick. We had Huddersfield fans inside the pub and groups of Bradford fans outside. All of a sudden people outside started hurling bricks through the windows, and fans inside responded by picking up bar stools and throwing them back." A police spokesman said around 60 arrests were made during the day with 35 of them taking place at Valley Parade."

Steff

Huddersfield (H)
22/03/86
FOR this game we decided to give Huddersfield a nasty surprise and go over to their place on the morning of the match despite the game being played at Odsal Stadium in Bradford. There was well over a 100 who met in the Interchange at 10.00 am. The first double decker bus was rammed to capacity and set off on the short 12 mile trip. Others went through in cars and vans. When the bus arrived we all headed up their boozer, The Crescent. As we got round the corner a small mob of Town were outside the pub waiting to get in. They got a right fucking shock when they saw us coming up the road. A few stood for a bit but they all legged it when they realised they didn't stand a chance.

Unfortunately the old bill were on us immediately as they had been keeping an eye on what the Town lads were up to. They weren't expecting us lot to turn up though. We were rounded up and put on buses back to Bradford. The police kept us sat on two double deckers outside Odsal for 3 hours until the game kicked off. Some of the City lads convinced a copper that on the radio it said the game was being played at Huddersfield and that's why we went over. He seemed to believe it. It's a shame we didn't arrive in Huddersfield when the pubs had opened as it would have been very interesting. I heard after, one of their main lads had been let out of jail the night before the game and they were all out and about.

Paul Durrant

ABOUT 20 of us had missed the lads in the Interchange so we caught a later bus to Huddersfield. This was in the days before mobile phones so when we got there we had no idea where the rest of the lads were. I now know they had already been rounded up and taken back to Bradford. So we are walking through the centre of Huddersfield when 'bang', about an 80 strong Town mob are charging down the street towards us. We didn't stand a chance and we legged it. They were breathing down our necks and looking for blood. I was never the fastest runner and this day I was wearing a sheepskin jacket which was slowing me down. But in other ways it saved me. A police van screeched to a halt in the road and thank fuck the Town lads gave up the chase. I'm bent over out of breath when one of the lads said: "Paul you've been sliced down the back."

They had been that close one had managed to run a blade down my back. I was lucky just to get a scratch as it had gone through the sheepskin and my jumper. I have a permanent scar on my back but it could have been much worse had the old bill not arrived. This sergeant is going mad asking what we were doing in Huddersfield and stuff. They escort us to a taxi rank and we head to a place called

Brighouse, which is a town between Bradford and Huddersfield. We got out of the taxis and had a wander before going into this boozer. Bad move. The place is packed with more Town lads and once again we are being attacked. This time we put up a bit of a fight but they had too many. Some of our lads barricaded themselves inside a video shop which got smashed to pieces by the Town lads. I hid in a petrol station and I could see 20 of the bastards looking about for me. I said to the man operating the petrol pump: "Please don't say a fucking word, they are looking for me."

Thankfully he didn't. I must have been there half-an-hour. I got another taxi back to Odsal and as soon as I got out of the car I landed in the middle of a brawl with City and Town at a roundabout. The numbers were much more to my liking this time though. What a day!

Mark

Huddersfield (A)
29/09/87
AFTER the Fire Disaster we had to play some of our games in Huddersfield and the younger lads always ended up having a row with black lads from over there. Some of them were part of the football mob but most were kids from the predominantly West Indian Fartown area. They used to come over to a club in Bradford called Time & Place and it would kick-off with them there too. It got to a point where something would happen every week. It was nothing to do with race. They seemed to hate the black lads with us the most.

None of the old Ointment were involved, it was just the younger lads who called themselves 'Section 5' or the 'Panel Beaters' in those days. A few of our lads like Crowy,

Chalky, Abbot and Cody were from Batley and Dewsbury. These are towns nearer Huddersfield than Bradford, and they would be in the thick of it as they knew some of the Town lads.

I remember going over to Huddersfield for this game. A few of us went on the bus and I was excited about what lay in store as we had battered these Fartown lads the weekend before. Being over enthusiastic as usual, I jumped off the bus when we arrived in Huddersfield expecting everyone to follow me. But I got off a stop too early and was on my own. I thought "Fucking hell I could be in trouble". I was right in the middle of where they all lived. As I'm walking down the street I noticed a black kid who was always fighting with us. He didn't see me but I spotted he was carrying a pair of adidas jeans trainers in his hands. I just knew something was not right about it and I had a bad feeling. After about ten minutes I caught up with the rest of the lads. They had been ambushed and one lad, Shane, had been taken down by a few of them. He was stabbed and had his adidas jeans removed from his feet. I had just come face-to-face with the kid who had done it. Later on, we were in a boozer called The Railway and Town's mob came and smashed all the windows. We all went out of the back door tooled up with tables and chairs and had it with them in the car-park and on the street. It was fucking mental for a few minutes as beer glasses, tables, pool cues, stools and bottles were being used as weapons. Eventually the Town lads fucked off and we got off too before the old bill arrived.

The place was littered with broken furniture and the locals were taking the good stuff into their houses. After the game, we came out in small groups and never got organised properly. Some of our lot went for a wander and were chased around the streets by black lads with machetes. One kid who used to knock about with us was almost deaf.

He was with a couple of Ointment lads hid in a bush as these black lads were looking for blood just yards away. They were holding their breath because they were in serious danger. But just as these tooled up lads go past, their cover was blown when this deaf kid shouts at the top of his voice: "Have they gone yet?"

Luckily they got picked up by a City lad who spotted them being chased up a dimly lit street. After what happened to Shane earlier on, it's not hard to work out what the consequences of being caught would have been.

Huddersfield (H)
24/09/94

FIGHTING before this game led to the largest number of Ointment members being sent to prison for one incident. Disturbances broke out at the Piste Bar on Manchester Road, Bradford, after Huddersfield's HYC mob were found to be drinking inside. Over 100 Ointment members attacked the pub unaware the police were filming the whole incident from across the street. Traffic on the busy dual carriageway was brought to a halt as Ointment members carried out wave after wave of attacks on the Piste Bar.

Operation Argo was launched by the police to capture those involved. Two months later scores of doors were kicked down in Bradford and Huddersfield in a series of dawn raids.

Fourteen Ointment lads and one HYC member were eventually jailed for between six months and two years for violent disorder or affray. While three others were given community service orders. The police were jubilant at the sentences dished out with one detective claiming in the local media: "The Ointment has never been dealt such a blow." One of the lads jailed for two years was 46 year-old 'Francis'.

Francis

I GOT into town about 11 am and headed straight to one of the pubs we used to meet in, The Queen. About 30 of us were having a chat over a beer about what might pan out over the day, pretty relaxed as Huddersfield's mob, the HYC, never showed up. But then to our surprise one of the lads came running in and tells us: "Town are up Manchester Road."

It turned out they were in a boozer called 'The Piste'. We drank up and made our way the half-a-mile towards them. Near the pub loads of road works were going on and the place was littered with iron poles meant for the ground work. They were too good to ignore so we all picked some up. As we approach the pub we spot the old bill outside so we drop our tools and just walk past the pub. The HYC lads came out for a look but nothing happened other than a few hand gestures and obscenities. We headed back into the city centre where another 80 or so Ointment had now gathered. Word got around the HYC were still in the Piste, so one of our lads went up to have a chat. When he came back he tells us good news (so we thought). The police had gone and Huddersfield were up for it. We made a brisk walk to the pub, armed to the teeth with bottles and bricks. As we see the HYC at the top of the steps, the "OINTMENT MENTAL" chant starts to flow out of our mouths. Bricks and bottles are thrown up the stairs forcing some of the HYC lads back into the pub only for them to re-emerge with reinforcements. As we make our way up the steps to the door of the pub small scuffles ensue and one of the Town lads is even game enough to get out of the door and take a swing at us. But outnumbered he's soon put to the floor and battered.

Whilst the fighting is going on someone shouted: "The coppers are filming us." Some of the lads cleared off, but in the heat of battle most just carry on regardless. We go back down the steps to give the HYC a chance to come out so we can have it good style with the cunts.

They come out throwing bottles, glasses, and buffets at us. We made a go for them but the loud sound of the sirens made most of our lads do a runner except for a few, including myself, who stayed for a little bit more. We never saw anything of Town for the rest of the day but we were all happy with the lunchtime shenanigans. But there was that niggling feeling of the police and the camera. No one was sure they wouldn't get an early knock in the future.

As feared, two months down the line twenty odd lads are dawn raided, three from Huddersfield and the rest from Bradford. We are all put on banning orders.

As the weeks and months go by City are doing well and some of the lads start to break the banning orders. We played Hull and were given the home end which resulted in pitch invasions and Hull being ran across their own stadium. For once I was a good boy and stayed on my banning order and listened to all the trouble live on radio while getting a tan under the sun bed.

It sounded good though, I wished I could have been there I thought to myself.

I then decided I just had to go into town later to see what the score was. One of the first lads I met was Scotty, minus an ear.

He told me this Hull lad just ran over to him and sunk his teeth into his ear and ripped it off. Scotty thought he had been punched until someone said "Your ear is missing."

As a year past we were up for sentencing for the Piste battle. Two of the HYC lads got off with it. The rest of us were found guilty or pleaded guilty to the charges. I remember the court room was full to bursting point.

I would say there was over 100 Ointment and family

there.

The sentences were read out and the lads were jailed for a total of 20 years. I got two years.

Judge Kent-Jones on watching the police video described the fighting as: "A scene from the Middle Ages or the Wild West."

Detective Inspector Phil Sedgwick, said Operation Argo had far-reaching consequences: "These were the leading members of Ointment who were highly involved in organising violence."

Steff

Wigan (A)
13/12/03
THIS is what they are the cunts. We'd been to Wigan, only about forty of us bothered to go over on the train as a load of our lads were on banning orders and others were just disillusioned with it. Anyhow, Wigan had chosen this as their big game of the season and they had a decent mob out as it happens but the old bill had us pretty much wrapped up as soon as we arrived. To be honest I heard Wigan had 150 out for us so maybe it was just as well. On the train home one of the lads got a call from a Huddersfield lad saying they were waiting in Halifax for our train to arrive and wanted to meet at a spot with no CCTV. Everyone was up for it but as soon as the train pulled in it was attacked by Town's firm. We couldn't even get off the train because of the shivering bastards. When something like that happens to a train it just fucking locks.

The Huddersfield Daily Examiner
"A MOB of soccer yobs ambushed a train and hurled missiles at the windows.

British Transport Police believe Huddersfield Town followers were to blame.

The train, which carried a mixture of Bradford City supporters and shoppers, was immediately taken out of service.

Police are appealing for information about the attack on the Manchester to York train as it pulled into Halifax Station at 10.30pm on Saturday night.

A group of about 30 men, believed to be Huddersfield Town supporters waiting on the platform, threw bricks and bottles. Eight windows were smashed.

Huddersfield Town played at Macclesfield on Saturday while Bradford's game was at Wigan.

A spokesman said officers were studying CCTV footage."

Ointment in Huddersfield 1983.

Chapter Fifteen

SPEAKING FROM THE SOUL CREW

ANYONE who has trawled book shelves looking for a read on football culture will recognise the name Annis Abraham Jnr. The Welshman and avid Cardiff City supporter, has written six books based on his love affair with his local football team. But it's his links with the infamous hooligan firm, the Soul Crew, which have thrust him into national limelight. The 47 year-old has been a key figure in the gang's activities stretching back three decades. The Soul Crew is regarded as one of the top mobs in the UK. Annis has also been subject to a BBC Panorama investigation into football hooliganism and has been tailed by reporters on a number of occasions. He is a household name in Wales. But that doesn't tell the whole story. In his younger days he helped his parents turn a rundown nightclub in Bradford, into one of the north's premier night spots. Caesars played host to some of the huge pop acts of the 80's including New Order, Big Country, Aswad and Marillion. It was during this time in Bradford that he became friends with members of the Ointment. He started to go to games with them and was involved in a number of clashes with rival hooligan gangs. However, his links with both Cardiff and Bradford, has resulted in physical attack and abuse from both sets of lads in the past. Annis Abraham's allegiance will always be with

Cardiff City and the Soul Crew. But here he gives an outsiders view of life inside the Bradford Ointment.

Annis

AS a13 year-old I got involved in the hooligan scene after being beaten up at a West Ham versus Cardiff game. I used to wear bleached jeans and Pringle jumpers and I looked about 18. The Cardiff lads accepted me and I loved going to the games and quickly got into the scene. But a couple of years later my dad announced that he had bought a rundown nightclub in Bradford and we would be moving up there. To be honest I didn't know much about Bradford. I'd heard about the Yorkshire Ripper and that's about it. So I moved up there with my parents but they had problems selling up in Cardiff and travelled back a lot. So I ended up having a hands on role at Tiffany's Nightclub in Bradford. I couldn't believe why they bought this place to be honest. But we changed the name to Caesars, and with hard work, it became very successful. By coincidence a few weeks after I moved up there in 1982, Bradford was due to play Cardiff away. They'd not played each other for about 40 years. So I went to Valley Parade to try and get a ticket on the supporter's bus down to Cardiff. I couldn't get one but there was a match taking place between Bradford and Oxford, and I decided to go in the Oxford end. I was dressed in my nice Pringle and stuff and I noticed a few lads stood nearby. I said to them: "You Oxford?"One of them replied: "No we're the Ointment."

Oxford didn't have anyone to fight so I got talking to these lads and they were alright with me. More and more came in and they mentioned the Ointment was taking a coach to Cardiff and I could come along. I thought to myself: "I've met the right lads already."

It was a Tuesday rainy night when we went down and I

was the youngest lad on the Ointment coach. It was the old Division Three and Bradford brought about 250 fans which wasn't bad for a game like that. I remember clubs at that time bringing 11 supporters to Cardiff on a Saturday. Everyone was good to me on the coach and there were no problems. I asked them to drop me off a mile from the ground so I could meet my mates and they did. There was no bother at the game and on the way home some of the Ointment told me they often went to Tiffany's. They used to come in on a Friday and Saturday night and I got to know them well. I also got to realise that at this time there was a decent number of Leeds fans in the Bradford area. In my opinion if I was from Bradford I wouldn't like it if people born and bred in the city supported Leeds. When I was at school in Cardiff it was full of Leeds and Liverpool fans and I hated them with a vengeance. So there was a lot of bother with Ointment lads kicking off with any Leeds fans they came across. I started to go to away games with Bradford and I was gobsmacked. They were taking 1500 fans to games in the north and I didn't expect that at all. I remember one of the older lads called Pete Newby. He was a real character who was always involved in fights at football. When they played Millwall for the first time in decades I was living in Bradford, and they were really up for this one. I was on my way to Wigan to see Cardiff and waiting at the train station in Bradford when some Millwall turned up. At the front was a lad from Cardiff who was now living in London and moving with the Millwall boys. He told me loads of Millwall's lads were on the next train. I decided to give Wigan a miss and went to tell the Ointment that Millwall were coming. I knew where to find the Bradford lads and within minutes a load of them had got to the train station. There was easy 150-200 waiting for that train to pull in. But fuck me. When Millwall got off the train there was just lads after lads walking along the platform.

The mob they brought to Bradford was huge. They burst through the line of police and there were battles going on all over. They were backing Bradford off and it was continuing all the way up to Mannigham Lane. I remember a Millwall lad at the front with a knife. At the ground I went into the seats with about 80-90 Ointment. We could not believe our luck as when we got in there was about 40 Millwall sat down with this prick from Cardiff along with them. The Ointment just ran into them and chased some Millwall onto the pitch. Later on Pete Newby ran across the pitch into the Millwall section and we were all cheering his name as he got dragged away by the police. Nothing much happened after the game as the place was flooded with police. Millwall might say they got the better of Bradford that day. But let's be honest about it. Millwall were in the top three in the country at the time. When they turned up they were better than just about anybody. Sadly Pete Newby has passed away.

There was loads of trouble in Bradford when they played Cardiff in 1983. And I got the blame, and I mean blame, by some Cardiff after nine of my mates got beaten up at the train station. I'd taken some Bradford lads to Sheffield United a few weeks before and when they saw that 400 Cardiff lads had come from Wales on the service train they were very impressed. So they had loads out expecting a big mob to arrive. The match at Bradford kicked-off on a Wednesday afternoon because one of the floodlights had been blown down. So it goes without saying not the usual numbers made the trip up north. I went to the game alone and left early to meet some lads who had come from Cardiff to see me. As I walked   away from the ground one of the big names in the Ointment came up to me and asked: "Where's your fucking Soul Crew?"

Then he smacked me in the face and fucked off. A lot of the younger Bradford lads said sorry to me and said it was out of order. It wasn't going to stop me going to Bradford games though. I went to Doncaster a few weeks later and Pete Newby put his arm around me and told me not to bother what anyone said and fair play for coming. It actually came on top for me at Doncaster near the ground but Bradford took the mick that day in Doncaster. But they did at most Yorkshire clubs. I used to try and explain it to Cardiff lads that wherever Bradford went in Lancashire or Yorkshire there would have a minimum of 1500-2000 supporters, and 150 lads. They were too big for the lower divisions. That was the thing with Bradford. The Ointment travelled as far away as Pompey in decent numbers when I lived there. I've spoken to a lot of Portsmouth lads and they respected Bradford in the day and would turn out for them home and away. Another time was when Bradford played at Huddersfield in 1984. The rivalry between the two was massive then. We went on the train and got there at 11 am.

Huddersfield all turned out for this one, but to be honest with you, they could not compete with Bradford. I'm not going to slate Huddersfield because they can pull good numbers themselves and they always turn out for Cardiff. But that day they just could not cope with what Bradford had out. People down south just didn't realise how good Bradford were. People went on about Leeds and all the lads they had. But Bradford lads all knew each other and you can't beat that. I know Leeds have taken the mick in city centres across the country but they can't say they have in Bradford. I'll never forget the time they played Manchester United in the cup. It was a two legged affair and both United and Bradford turned out for it. There was loads of fighting in the city centre and Valley Parade. After the match all the Bradford lot went to the train station and we surged up the escalators towards the United lads on the platform. It was going off big style and the lad next to me became my best mate in Bradford, Paul MacKenzie. I met some very good lads and I will never forget them. We might not have been the main Ointment at the time but we went with them and we had some good times. The best times. Sadly I lost contact with a lot of these friends due to moving about the country. But because of Facebook I've got back in touch with some Bradford lads and in May 2012, I was invited up for the last game of the season against Swindon and took a mate with me. They were also having a photo shoot for the book. In this day and age with bans and all the stuff to keep lads away from football it hasn't stopped the camaraderie at Bradford. There must have been 200-250 lads turned out for this game and they were sound with us. I was gobsmacked to see so many faces from the past. Some have sadly died, but my old mucker Paul MacKenzie was there.

I went past my old nightclub and was sad to see it all boarded up. I'm being straight and I'm not making Bradford out to be super men, because they weren't. But they are as a good a set of lads you will meet anywhere in the country.

When I left Bradford in 1984 I was gutted because it was a rough and edgy place and I enjoyed living there. When I got back to Cardiff some people accused me of being too friendly with the Bradford lot. But you take people as you find them. They looked out for me. I've said before that I came to Bradford a boy, and left a man. I remember Bradford came to Cardiff in 1993, and I kept out of the way. The Ointment turned up at the Owain Glyn Or pub which was where the Soul Crew lads went for a pint. They barged in and one of them hit a good mate of mine and told him to get the riot gear on because Ointment was here. It was a shock for my mate as he usually got the first punch in. They had a right old mob in there. When Cardiff got its act together the police were about and everything. I'll tell you there are only six or seven teams who have gone into our city centre in the last 30-40 years. Bradford got a lot of respect for that and Cardiff lads haven't forgotten. We played Bradford away later that season and the Soul Crew went over big time. They took coaches to Halifax, then went the rest of the way by train. Again I had to keep out of it and went up in the car. Many people are saying Cardiff got the better of Bradford that day. Before the game I kept a low profile and went to the ground. Afterwards I walked the other way when it was all kicking off. I just want to say RIP to Manny. He was a good Bradford lad who is no longer with us.

Waiting for Cardiff outside the away end in 1994.

Town Boys in action. Bradford City v Southampton Valley Parade F.A.
Cup 6th March 1976. *Copyright the Telegraph and Argus, Bradford.*

Meatmen 1982. John Hammond (RIP), White Toddy, Whitehead,
Dave Smith, Rikki D, Tony Wright and Black Toddy.

Young Bradford Ointment before Swindon 2012.

Some of the older lads before Swindon at home 2012.

Bradford Ointment in Leeds city centre three hours
before Carling Cup match in 2011.

Leeds Service Crew and Ointment clash in Leeds city centre 2011.

Stockport town centre left trashed. Six Ointment members were jailed following these clashes.

Former night-club doorman Paul Durrant has seen it all over the years.

A Rangers ICF member about to get smacked in the mouth during clashes with the Ointment in 2002.

Oldham 1989. Bradford lads running Oldham
through their own town centre.

Paul Whitehead and Phil Dunne are two well known Ointment faces.

Panel Beaters on the road in the late 80's.

Ointment and Leeds Service Crew clash before game
at Odsal in 1986.

TOP. Gilly, Sean Durrant(RIP) and Chris McCarthy ready for Leeds in 1986.
BELOW. Ointment waiting in Newby Square for Leeds to show.

TOP. Bradford and Leeds clash in Newby Square.

BELOW. Ointment heading to Red Ginn after running Leeds down Manchester Road.

TOP. Ointment lads head towards the Leeds Service Crew.

BELOW. Police Hoolivan films the Ointment before Leeds game in 1986.

Some well known faces outside Andy Naylor's van in 1981.

Ointment at Carlisle in 1985 with Pete Newby (RIP) on the far-right in sleeveless jumper. Manny (RIP) in the shades.

Young Bradford Ointment in 2009.

Dean, Paul D, Cums, Tiny, Noddy and Chris C
amongst others in the 80's.

Chapter Sixteen
BATTLE WITH THE BLADES

SHEFFIELD United hit hard times in the early 80's and found themselves in Division Four. It was the start of the casual scene and the Blades Business Crew (BBC) was the first big mob to come to Bradford dressed in smart gear. Clashes between the Ointment and the BBC were extremely violent. One City fan was killed after being hit by a car during running battles near Odsal Stadium, while a number of Ointment members have been jailed for incidents with Blades supporters. The rivalry has continued with good turn outs and a heavy police presence guaranteed when the two clubs meet.

Sheffield United (H)
24/10/81

Chris
THIS was going to be a big game for the Ointment. Sheffield United had a very good reputation and had been in the top divisions having it with the so-called elite and holding their own. We knew they would pay us a visit and we were ready.

In those days the local paper would tell you on a Friday what time the football specials were coming in so we knew when Sheffield would be arriving. It was not unusual for hooligans to come on the football specials along with the 'normal' supporters. We had loads out in a pub called the Painted Wagon just a few hundred yards from the train station. We felt we were about to really test ourselves with a big club with a big reputation. This was the sort of fixture the Ointment had been starved of. We had a few hundred out for this game and by this time I was really into the hooligan stuff. There were a load of pool tables in the Painted Wagon and they were cleared as lads took a ball each ready to throw. When Sheffield came out of the Interchange the police took them towards Broadway and past the Telegraph & Argus building where we were waiting to ambush them. We steamed into the escort and pool balls and glasses were flying into them. It was during this incident I first got hit by a truncheon and it hurt. From here on, the whole day was just fighting and there were loads of arrests. There was a mass brawl all along Manningham Lane after the Ointment attacked Sheffield near a pub called the Royal Standard. I remember one lad had a Sheffield kid by the hair in the middle of the road and they were both hit by a police car. The Sheffield lad's head hit the car's radiator grill and blood splattered all over the bonnet. It looked shocking but the lad got up. In the ground the terracing was falling to bits and the concrete was used as ammunition to throw over at the away supporters on the other side of the fence. At the Sheffield game I'd never seen so many people walking about with bleeding heads as a barrage of rocks, golf balls, darts and more went backwards and forwards throughout the game.

Considering they were supposed to be one of the best mobs around at the time we gave as good as we got, no question about it.

Telegraph & Argus:

"Furious Bradford City fans stoned police after a club record eluded their team. Tempers flared as City supporters, hoping their team would break a club record of nine successive league victories at Valley Parade on Saturday, went 2-0 down to Sheffield United. The ugly scenes brought a warning from Bradford police today that soccer hooligans would face a tough no-nonsense line in future. Supt. Bernard Burke, of Central Division said: "Enough is enough." He spoke as a young police officer lay in hospital after being hit in the back with a brick. His condition is said to be satisfactory. Police arrested 62 fans, mainly teenagers, for public order offences. Fifty six of the arrests were made inside the ground. Earlier 120 police shepherded 4,500 Sheffield United fans from the Interchange to three special trains. They were stoned by Bradford City supporters in Thorncliffe Road. During the match concrete blocks were thrown across the terraces. About £200 damage was caused to the Theatre Tavern pub. United fans used the pub while City fans drank next door in the Royal Standard. Landlady Valerie Firth said: "A row started outside and they just smashed the place up. They were throwing glasses and ashtrays at everybody. They went berserk."

Supt Burke called for sterner sentences.

"The way I see it, a lot of these people aren't here to watch football but are here to confront opposing fans and the police. We are in the middle of it and going to have to take a firmer line. More men will be on duty and there are going to be arrests. We cannot have decent people going to watch football being hampered by what I call low class hooligans. If they are going to come looking for trouble they will get it. We have had enough of it. We are not having policemen injured under these circumstances."

Bradford City secretary Terry Newman said: "I have heard of no reports of police being stoned or concrete blocks being thrown and I think people are inclined to exaggerate."

Sheffield United (H)
08/05/83

Jimmy

FOR me, Sheffield United are one of the best to come to Bradford as they hardly ever fail to show and are always up for it. At this game I went down to the Unicorn where the lads used to meet up and was chatting to a few who I sort of knew from seeing at matches. I'd still only got to know a few of the Ointment at this point. There were only about 20 in as the main City mob had met up in a different pub on the edge of town. I'd not been in long when word got round Sheffield's Blades Business Crew (BBC) was in The Queen pub near the train station. We headed up for a look but they spotted us first. Suddenly there were 100 lads charging down the road towards us. Fuck this. We backed off as far as the bottom of Ivegate when one of the kids I was with turned around and steamed straight into them. I couldn't just leave him so a few of us stopped running and had a go with the BBC. We were well outnumbered and if the old bill had not come within a minute or two we would have got seriously done in. The lad who initially ran into them had his nice Pringle ripped to shreds. All he said was:

"I enjoyed that."

I got to know him well. His name was Chris Pickles.

Leicester Forest
03/05/86

Chris

WE were on our way to Portsmouth and set off from Bradford in the early hours. Only one coach left at that time but it was full of decent lads. Everyone had been out drinking on the Friday so we were all pissed before we even set off. The police in Bradford were on to us so we ended up playing cat-and-mouse with them in the city centre to get on the coach without them knowing. We ended up hiding down an alley and arranged for the coach to come and get us at the entrance. By the time we got to Leicester Forest at about 2.30 am we had just finished watching the violent film 'Warriors' on the TV. When we were getting off we noticed a mob of other lads getting off a coach and it wasn't long before it kicked off. It turned out it was Sheffield United's Blades Business Crew on the way down to Crystal Palace. What added to the violence that was to follow was work was being carried out on the car-park at Leicester Forest and the place was littered with concrete blocks, metal poles, signs and all sorts of stuff to use in a battle. Sheffield started bouncing about and the Ointment steamed straight into them. A cocky big black lad of theirs at the front with an apple in his mouth got smacked straight in the face and ended up with a broken jaw. More of the BBC came out of the service station throwing bottles and City sent the building stuff flying back at the BBC. They eventually started to back off before running like fuck over the motorway. One of their lads ended up with a fractured skull after being smashed over the head with a concrete slab. The Ointment got back on the coach and told the driver to leave. But as we were pulling out of the services a brick came flying through the back window so we all got off again. But blue lights were flashing everywhere and the cops had arrived in force. The whole coach got arrested and taken to Wigston Police Station. The front page of the Leicester Mercury described in its headline the next day as "Wild West Battle" and that is exactly what it was like.

Leicester Mercury:
"Forty-six Bradford City supporters were detained for questioning following the clash in which bricks, bottles, metal bars and fists flew. Two men were seriously injured and taken to Leicester Royal Infirmary. One man who was believed to have been hit in the face with a brick, suffered a broken jaw, and another who was hit over the head with a blunt instrument has a fractured skull. Neither of the men, both from Sheffield, have yet been named by the police."

In the interviews a lot of the lads blamed the coach driver for putting the Warriors film on the telly and getting everyone in a violent mood.

Some lads got charged and ended up getting jail sentences of up to two-and-a-half years.

Paul Whitehead
I GOT the coach from a firm that specialised in children's trips and we booked it for midnight. Everyone was tanked up and we spent a while trying to give the police the slip in Bradford before we set off. The driver was horrified when he saw who was getting on his coach. He thought he was taking school kids to a boating regatta on the Isle of Wight. The coach was strictly five star with a toilet, video screens, etc. One of the lads, Cough, brought the film Warriors that he had hired and we started to watch it. The film was just finishing when we pulled into Leicester Forest. After the brawl the whole coach was arrested and escorted to a police

station in Leicester. The police did not start letting us out until the Portsmouth game had kicked-off so we couldn't get to the game. By this time the driver had gone back. For the next few weeks I was getting hassle from the coach company looking for money for the broken window, and Cough wanting the Warriors video back. I never managed to get a coach from this company again. Cough rang me out of the blue too, to tell me to forget about the Warriors video. When I asked if he had got it back, he replied:

"No, the bloke at the video shop is dead."

Chapter Seventeen

CRUISING AND BRUISING FOR ENGLAND

OVER the years lads from Bradford have travelled across the world to follow England. They have been at the forefront of some of the most infamous battles on the international stage. From the early 80's they were prepared to wage war for their beloved country against like minded foreigners or over-zealous police forces. Every major tournament for 30 years has been attended by members of the Ointment. Many of the scrapes they were involved in were seen through the haze of LSD, E's and cocaine. On some occasions they were left to fight for their lives in hostile environments. But the scene has changed in recent times with international bans taking a toll. The numbers of those prepared to put their neck on the line in distant lands has diminished greatly. The English disease has to a great extent been cured. But for many Bradford lads, travelling abroad to watch England play, it was more than just blind patriotism. It was about having a laugh with your mates. Here, some of the lads recall some of their most memorable moments on England duty.

Luxembourg
European Championship Qualifier
16/11/83

Chris

MYSELF and Javo went over to Amsterdam first on Persil washing powder tickets. A lot of firms travelled on the service train to games because Persil had a 2 for 1 offer with British Rail at the time. They also did a special offer for European Five Day breaks and that's what we went on. From Amsterdam we got the train down to Luxembourg the day before the match. In those days not a lot of City lads bothered with England games. We had no digs, and ones that had space would not let us in. And like hundreds more English, we had no tickets for the game. There were loads of England fans with no place to stay hanging about getting pissed. We were only eighteen at the time so it was a big adventure for me and Javo. We were sat in a cafe wondering what we were going to do and then this group of Scousers come bouncing in with all the latest clobber on. It was the first time I'd seen a firm in Fila, Tachinni, etc and it looked great. They all looked like the characters from the Harry Enfield Show but in those days it looked pretty cool.

They went up to the counter and bang, one of them smacked the owner and that was it. The tills went, cigs got taken, they cleared the cafe and fucked off back out. It was the first time I'd seen the robbing side to it. We were still eating our fucking dinner and all this was going on around us. One of the Scousers on his way out carrying a load of smokes said: "The bizzees will be coming, you better fucking run lads." We just took our steak with us and cleared off. We ended up boozing around Luxembourg with the other English fans before the police shepherded us all down to the railway station. We found a spot to bed down in the toilet among the England fans and local druggies. On the day of the match we went back on the piss. We spotted the Scousers a few more times robbing sports shops, supermarkets and jewellers. That's all they were doing.

Talking to a few they were using England games at the time as cover for robbing. Good luck to them. We were the daft cunts paying for everything. There was no one to fight in Luxembourg other than the police and they didn't have a clue. They used Range Rovers when they arrested people and they just got smashed up as they had no protection. We managed to get a couple of tickets off these English lads during the day and got to the ground. Inside about 50 Sheffield United had got into the home section and were scrapping with Luxembourg fans and the police but they left them in there. During the game we just took the piss.

The toilets got wrecked and everything in it was thrown at the police. Everything you could get your hands on was just launched at the police who had lost complete control. They were just lined up like target practice or a fair ground attraction. England won the game 4-0 but other results meant we had failed to qualify for the European Championships and that added fuel to what was already a powder keg. The police tried to keep us in and some Luxembourg had come to the gates taunting us. But by this time the Sheffield lads had come round and they just fired into them. That was it then. We stormed the gates and everyone was going proper mental. Any car in our way was getting turned over. I never realised how easy it was to turn a car but three hyped up lads could do it no problem. The police had just lost it. In Luxembourg they had dust bins like we have today and they were just lined up in streets waiting to be emptied. There were hundreds of them and they were launched through shop windows and at the cops.

One went through a jeweller's window and in front of

me was a tray of rings that someone had dropped when running off. But by this time the authorities had drafted in the army and Luxembourg was actually an undefended country for a few hours as the soldiers had all been drafted in to deal with us lot. I was just about to pick the tray of rings up when the army came running down the street getting stuck in with their batons. I was gutted. With the army the gloves had come off. They meant business and were cracking skulls so we all fucked off quick. I ended up in a boozer with this lad from Hull called Jacko, who invited me back to this hotel where all the Hull lads were stopping.

I was chuffed as I'd not slept for a few days. About four of us got a taxi back to this hotel and to be honest the talk was of rolling the taxi driver. We started arguing about the fare when we got there but then a load of police appeared and got stuck straight into us with these rubber truncheons that killed. But fair play to the taxi driver he was screaming at the police to stop and we paid him and they fucked off. By this time I had lost Javo so I went back to the train station and found him before we both headed back to the hotel where the Hull lads were stopping. When we went back it turned out Jacko had been nicked but another Hull lad said we could get our heads down on the floor. The place was like a doss house and we went straight to sleep with dozens more. During the night and unknown to us, the cops had kicked doors down in the hotel and nicked a few more but we slept through it. The owner was going mental wanting people to pay for the damage as the place was a right mess. We quietly slipped away and got to the train station. All bags were searched because of all the looting. An amazing experience that trip - I'll never forget it.

BBC news report:

"More than 20 English football supporters have been arrested in Luxembourg after a night of violence. The fans are being held for drunkenness, fighting and stealing after England was knocked out of the European Championship in spite of beating Luxembourg. Denmark's victory over Greece earlier on Wednesday meant England finished second in their group and do not qualify for the finals next year. The fans were not placated by a 4-0 win over Luxembourg and trouble started inside the stadium during which two police officers were badly hurt. Afterwards England supporters raced through the city centre overturning cars and smashing shop windows. About 500 police officers and 150 soldiers were on duty in an attempt to head off trouble. They were hoping to prevent a repeat of violent disturbances in 1977 when England fans also ran riot. But the omens had not been good with trouble flaring before many of the 2,000 fans even reached their destination. On Tuesday about 20 English men beat up a railway employee in Belgium and four police officers needed hospital treatment after fighting broke out among drunken fans who got off a ferry in Ostend. At the height of Wednesday night's violence riot police from neighbouring West Germany had to be drafted in to help the over-stretched Luxembourg forces. Weapons seized included axes and aerosol cans filled with tear gas. Many England supporters spent the night on the streets because local hotels refused to take them in. Finally they were herded to the railway station by the security forces where a train, brought forward by five hours, was waiting to take them to the ferry port in Ostend, Belgium. Those arrested are being kept in custody overnight and are expected to appear in court tomorrow."

Germany
European Championship 1988

Dean

THERE were 10 or so of us over there. We first had trouble with the Germans in Stuttgart. They were a scruffy bunch who looked like bikers. There were loads of lads from all over England and we took the piss in Stuttgart and ran them all over. The biggest thing about Stuttgart was we met some lads from Liverpool, Rory, Snozzer and Wog were three. These friendships would eventually change the ecstasy dance scene in Bradford and West Yorkshire forever. But that's another book entirely. So when we moved on to Düsseldorf I was expecting the same sort of thing. I had it in my mind that the Germans didn't have any lads, just a rabble of pissed up heavy metal locals. All the England fans were hanging about the train station and word got round in Düsseldorf that the Germans were coming for a show at 9 pm. I was only 19 at the time and ended up on ITV's 'This Week' programme that was covering the hooligan problem in Germany. I'd rang my mother up to check with things at home and she went mad down the phone saying that she had just finished watching Coronation Street and I appeared on the telly straight after. It was a really hot day and all the England lads had been hanging around waiting for this so-called German super firm to turn up. We thought even if they did come they would be a load of knobs. There were about 600 England fans in the square near the station and about 200 of those were lads. Then as the bell chimed on stroke of 9pm on the train station clock, about 1,000 Germans appeared inside the station. A load of trains arrived at the same time full of the cunts. They all had all the latest football gear. They looked like a huge English mob, they even had some black lads with them all chanting:

"Deutschland Hooligans." We had dealt with black leather jacketed rockers in Stuttgart but this lot were completely different. The English scarfer piss heads started to drift away. The train station had a big supermarket attached to it. So us, West Ham and some Scousers ran through the supermarket to get at the Germans in the station. The Scousers lagged behind as they were robbing. When we got through, the Germans had disappeared but I knew with a mob that size they had not fucked off. By this time the supermarket is empty apart from 300 England thugs who are robbing everything. Some were celebrating that we had run the Germans. But ten minutes later I was proved right.

Like a scene from Zulu, they all appeared on this side street. It looked like there were 3,000 of them this time. The West Ham lads at the front were gobby bastards and treating it as if it was West Ham versus the Germans. They were game but we put them straight that it was fuck all to do with West Ham. At the front of the German mob was this big black lad who was dressed just like an English thug. I was looking at him with respect thinking I'd like to have a pint with him later on. The Germans let off CS gas and to be honest the England firm was backing off. There was a lot of building work going on around the station with scaffolding and stuff lying about. I picked a pole up and launched it into the Germans. The English seemed to be back on the ball when I did that and we started to get on top until eventually this huge mob of Germans legged it. But the night was not over as they kept on coming back in smaller mobs and English lads were brawling non-stop for about six hours.

The police had just lost control. Afterwards me and a lad called Muddy were walking over the river in Dusseldorf on this huge bridge, a bit like the Humber Bridge, that seemed to go on forever. About a quarter-of-a-mile over we spotted this mob coming towards us. I asked Muddy if he could swim and he said he couldn't so I told him if he ends up in the water he was to get on my back. We were worried as this wall of people got closer and the drop into the water was fucking huge. Thank fuck it was not German thugs but a load of old people. Had it been their mob we would have been thrown over I have no doubt about that. There was huge tension in town and the Germans were up for it.

Scotland (A)
17/05/ 89

Dean

THIS was short lived trip. I hired a mini-bus from a place called Rent-A-Wreck in Bradford. I left £20 and a leather jacket as a deposit. There were about 15 of us on board. But when I went round the first roundabout the van went over on its side. We climbed out and the thing was fucked. We turned it back over and pushed it behind some flats and went on the piss. It turned out be a mad day up there with loads of English lads taking the piss. There was still a good few from Bradford there. But that's a chance you took with Rent-A Wreck. It was a Bradford institution at the time and well used by the Ointment. We once took a pensioners bus with a lift on the back to Wigan full of lads.

SWEDEN
Tor Brittania.
06/09/89

Dean

THERE were about 25 of us and about the same Middlesbrough on the boat. We had the biggest mobs with all the rest having between half-a-dozen and a dozen. Everyone was getting on at first. We were all going to

Sweden and we were going to smash them to pieces. No problem. Altogether there were 400 England fans on the boat and they were lads. As the fare was only £99, most were mainly tight-fisted northern lads, but there was a scattering of others such as West Ham. The boat was also awash with E's and acid tabs. The trouble started when we were all in the Concert Room. The Captain of the ship was a silly cunt from Denmark. He was meeting and greeting people and stuff like that. Well, for whatever reason he got hold of a microphone and appeared on stage. He then burst into song blaring out: "Maybe it's because I'm a Londoner, that I love London town." There were hardly any southerners on the boat never mind Cockneys. That was it. The boat just exploded. Bottles were flying and people started fighting with each other and this was the start of it.

Boro caused a lot of the bother on this trip by picking on smaller firms on board such as Rotherham. At the beginning we were talking to them and getting on but they had started on everyone else and they eventually turned on us. The difference with us though, was we had a good tight mob on the boat that knew we would give it to them. The other lads aboard knew something would happen with us and Boro. You would hear them talking about it. Eventually this huge Boro lad with a bald head was in this foyer area. He's shouting at the top of his voice he was sick of Bradford and he was going to kill us and shit like that. One of the lads with me was a kid called Gervais. Sadly he passed away a couple of years back. He was from a Gypsy background and was probably one of the hardest lads in Bradford at the time. He fought bare-knuckle fights at Appleby Horse Fair and stuff like that. He knocked about with us lot for a few years. One-on-one, he was a hard cunt.

So I said to my mates, Tommy and Gervais "Let's walk through." I could see Gervais was wound up a bit so I told him just to concentrate on the big fella and not worry about what's going on around. Anyway this big skinhead Boro lad comes barging through everyone to me, Gervais and Tommy. "Right you Bradford wankers, I'm fucking sick of you. I'll fight any of you cunts," he calls. I told Gervais to bang this cunt with all he had. And by fuck he did. Just as he cracked him the boat keeled over. As this big skinhead goes over, his mates who were behind him at these heavy glass doors, also went over. As the doors swung open they all fell through. It looked like he knocked about twenty of them over. He could not have timed his punch better. We never saw Boro again all night. They stayed well below deck. So we had a situation on board where Boro ran the lower deck and we ran the upper deck. Lads from other clubs were deciding who they should go with, us or them.

Fights were kicking-off all over the place. Meanwhile in the casino, the croupier had lost it. One of ours, Francis, was placing his chips on the number the ball landed on and the croupier was too scared to do anything about it. He eventually fucked off screaming that Francis was winning too much. Soon after a lad from Plymouth who we had been mates with jumped over board and his body was never found. Tragic. We had been getting on with these Plymouth lads, although the kid who jumped was actually a Leeds fan.

We once went down to Plymouth and got a puncture just as a load of Plymouth's firm, Central Element, were coming up the road. We were surrounded by them. But fair play they helped us change the tyre and let us go on our way. When we got on the ship I recognised one or two of them so we got on. There was loads of acid going about and confusion everywhere. Boro lads had let off all the fire extinguishers in the lower deck and this Plymouth lad had by all accounts thought the ship was on fire and jumped. When we heard about this we went looking for Boro and gave them a kicking. We ended up running the ship and to be honest we spent half the time trying to steady things down. For about two hours there was complete chaos on the boat. In one of the bars a DJ was trying to calm everyone down saying it was cool and telling everyone to have a good time. But when he was not looking he got spiked with a handful of acid tabs. An hour later he was singing: "Engerland, Engerland" and "Let's go fucking mental!"After a bit we noticed there was no staff about. Eventually an announcement came over that the ship was being abandoned as the staff had lost control of the ship. I looked out of the window and there was fucking loads of the ship's crew getting into a helicopter. The DJ was being winched up in a stretcher. We sussed out by now the boat was turning back. Some of the lads did not believe we were heading back until they spotted about 500 police in British uniforms standing by the dock. We got off and everyone was made to sit down in this huge room at Harwich. The police wanted to know what happened to the Plymouth lad who jumped. We were all eventually released and even got a letter of apology from the shipping company and received a full refund.

HOLLAND (Rotterdam)
World Cup Qualifier
13/10/93

Chris
THE authorities had made a big thing about stopping English thugs getting to this game but still one ferry company put on a cheap deal from Harwich to Amsterdam the day before the England match. So a good little mob of us got tickets and drove down. Of course the ferry was jammed solid with England fans. We got searched going on

but it did not stop the ferry being rife with E's. Not often would that happen on a ferry going to Amsterdam. Surprisingly there was little bother on the journey over. We arrived in the morning and there were a few fights going off here and there with the Dutch through the day but nothing much. Word had got round that Holland were up for it and it was all going to kick off at 10pm. But we thought nothing of it. By this time there is about ten or so Ointment in a bar when bang on 10 pm, we hear this commotion outside the bar we were in. We went outside and it's kicking off all over the place. We steamed straight into what we thought was Holland's lads. But fuck sake it was plain clothed cops. They pulled the batons out and were hammering us down this side alley but thank fuck they did not seem bothered about arresting us as it was kicking off all around us. The Dutch lads were on their toes and it was England fans and the police that were at it with each other. There must have been a thousand lads at it with the old bill.

All the café bars and sex shops closed because of the violence and this was the first time this had happened since World War Two. As the night wore on everything shut down. England fans that had hotels started to disappear.

The place became eerie, like a ghost town. It seemed we were the only English about on the streets. We had nowhere to stay and it became increasingly dodgy walking around Amsterdam in the early hours. There were little groups of slimy cunts all over giving us daggers and you could sense something bad was in the air. Anyway eventually this cunt came over and started to give one of our lads called Scotty a bit of grief. I said: "Smack the cunt," and Scotty replied: "You smack the cunt."

So I went to smack the cunt and he pulled a massive machete out and chased me and Scotty round a car. Thank fuck a couple of cops saw it and yanked him off but we knew we had to get out. We got to the train station and managed to get a train to Rotterdam at 4 am. We got there and loads of England fans started appearing including some more Ointment lads. It was big news on the TV about what had happened in Amsterdam and a few England fans had a pipe bomb thrown at them earlier in the day.

We were all knackered as we had not slept for a few days. In the evening Feyenoord and Ajax turned up but started having ago with each other so we just left them at it. Eventually they got their act together and turned up at a boozer we were in. We were first into the cunts and it was the first time I'd heard Ointment shouted at an international game. We were right at the front, a load of us, and we had some proper good lads with us. The Dutch were backing off when the police arrived. A load of Cockneys that were in the bar from various clubs hung around with us after that. We had no tickets but the police rounded us up and told us everyone would get into the game with or without a ticket.

We got to the ground and there were these long cages leading to the turnstiles. Those who had tickets went down one side of the cage and those without another side.

Anyway about 300 of us without tickets were told by the police we were nicked and we had to get on this line of buses that were waiting. Of course it kicked-off big time but the cunts were smashing us inside these cages with batons, whacking your fingers and stuff. Eventually we were put on the buses and taken to a military base and made to sit on the buses until the early hours. In the early hours they drove us back to the train station and threw us out. It was fucking freezing cold. The ferry terminal was about 40 minutes from the city centre and we set off looking for somewhere to sleep. Many England fans were kicking warehouse doors down, lighting fires or even wrapping themselves up in cardboard. By the time the ferry came in the morning everyone was well pissed off. Another night of no sleep.

ITALY (Rome)
World Cup Qualifier
11/10/97

Chris

WE flew over here and the old bill were bastards to start off with. They were always trying to provoke trouble. The day before the game we were having a beer in Rome and they just came over and took the drinks off everyone and smashed the bottles on the floor. They stared at us as if to say "What you going to do about it?" We got some digs this time and had no bother with anyone before the game. Some Chelsea lads were winding us up trying to get us to start on some Huddersfield lads. We bullied them a bit but nothing serious. A Sheffield BBC lad on his own tagged onto us and we also got friendly with some Arsenal lads who had a load of top notch whizz. On the day of the match we heard that England fans on their own had been stabbed but we got nothing. On the way to the ground it was bit of a free-for-all. Loads had tickets and loads were without. Cars were getting smashed up and shops robbed etc. We had tickets for the game as some of our lot were in the official England Travel Club. The police ended up putting everyone in a sort of no-man's land part of the ground even though we had tickets for the official away end. But they wanted to get people in the ground quick to stop the vandalism and stuff outside. As soon as we got in the Italians started pelting us with frozen bottles of water and unveiling IRA flags. So we started returning the bottles. The police were only interested in having a pop at us and this went on throughout the game. One England lad got hold of a copper and put his hand under his visor and tried to pull his helmet off. But he got a right whack on the head with a truncheon. He was well fucked, knocked straight unconscious. We managed to drag him back to where we all were. They kept us in for over an hour after the game before letting us out. We were right at the front and the England fans behind us were pelting the cops with missiles that were flying over our heads. Then the Carabinieri arrived. They are like a military police and a right set of bastards. About fifty of us got stuck in no man's land. They came flying in with sticks, rifle butts and bats and I put my arm up to protect my head. It's lucky I did because the cunts broke my arm such was the force of the blow. England fans were lying all over the street as the Carabinieri smashed them over their heads with rifle butts.

It's lucky no one got killed up that street. Eventually we got back to the hotel and then flew home. The day after my wife was taking me to hospital and the phone rang. It was one of the lads asking if I'd seen The Sun. It turned out I was on the front page involved in the chaos that was going on in the ground. Don't get me wrong a lot of England fans deserve it. But it's got to the stage now where anyone is liable to get a good hiding from the old bill at England matches in Europe. Even old men are targeted. It's all changed now, hardly any mobs of lads go. I would not recommend anyone to follow England abroad anymore. If the police don't batter you some slimy cunt will stick a blade in you. It's not worth it. A lot of the normal England fans want English hooligans back as they are the ones getting grief from the foreign thugs now. If you're English, you are fair game.

TURKEY (Sunderland)
European Championship Qualifier
02/04/03

Chris

I'VE never seen as many lads out for an England game as this. There was a lot of bad feeling leading up to this match stemming from the stabbing to death of two Leeds fans in Istanbul in 2000. Loads were just wandering about hoping to bump into Turkish fans hours before the game. Luckily for them they were not to be seen. Had they been around they would have got hammered. Fifteen of us went up in a mini-bus and met up with lads from all over the country.

Clubs such as Newcastle, Sunderland and Boro had decent firms out plus a good 200 Leeds Service Crew out for revenge on the Turks. For most of the day there had been an uneasy truce amongst the English lads with everyone's focus being on Turkey. However, as the day wore on the north-east firms started to have fall-outs and old rivalries started to surface. Some of us went with Boro lads to attack a pub full of Newcastle fans only to find that with the Newcastle mob were some other Ointment lads. Everyone was attacking each other really. The police were well on top of things as far as protecting the Turks was concerned. They were beating the English back with batons at every opportunity. As time wore on the Leeds lads were getting frustrated at not being able to have a pop at the Turks and started to get leery. And they turned their attention on to us. One of their lads who I know told me they knew we were in town and also knew where we had parked the bus. He warned us Leeds were planning to do us and he advised us to fuck off. There was no point hanging around as we would have stood no chance. It's not what we had come for anyway. But such is life, we got in the van and set off back home.

Chapter Eighteen
NATIONAL SERVICE

FOR many football fans in towns and cities across the country, the visit of Leeds United's Service Crew meant trouble. This group had one of the most active and largest hooligan firms around. It gained a notorious reputation throughout the 70's, 80's and 90's. Leeds had good numbers wherever they travelled due to the large fan base living outside the West Yorkshire city. There was another hooligan group named the Very Young Team but to avoid confusion they come under the label of Service Crew. Leeds regularly took mobs of 400 plus for big games.

On the other hand the city of Leeds itself can only boast average hooligan numbers. This is one factor why the Service Crew's dealings with the Bradford Ointment is not as straight forward as some may assume. It would be erroneous for Bradford lads to claim to have a similar nationwide reputation as that of Leeds. Nor could they claim to have regularly taken it to the biggest and best firms in the country like the Service Crew did. But Leeds thugs haven't always got their own way when facing the Ointment. Far from it. In the early 80's the only opportunity the Ointment had to have a go with Leeds was the pre-season West Riding Cup tournament. These games would be marred by violence and stabbing incidents. They no longer take place because of the huge policing costs.

The most high-profile league clash was when Leeds fans rioted at Odsal Stadium causing a chip van to burst into flames. However, that is by no means the whole story. Before and after this match the Ointment did very well against huge numbers and many were jailed. The Leeds United Service Crew has come seriously unstuck home and away against Bradford down the years.

Possibly no mob in the country has turned up more times in Leeds city centre than Bradford's. This includes on match days or pre-arranged meets when the Ointment has changed trains at Leeds. As recently as August 2011, more than 200 Bradford lads spent the afternoon drinking in Service Crew haunts, and running Leeds ragged before a Carling Cup match at Elland Road.

When the teams last met at Valley Parade, Leeds lads avoided Bradford altogether and headed for Shipley where they were wrapped up by the police. The Ointment had 300 lads in the city centre waiting.

There is no attempt to try and get one over the neighbours in this chapter. The notoriety the Service Crew has earned itself is well documented elsewhere and not contested. But this is what happened when they've come across Bradford.

Leeds United (H)
11/08/84

Steff

THIS was a Friendly match staged during the peak of football hooliganism in England. Leeds brought 400 plus lads over to Bradford. Fighting was breaking out all over the city centre from   opening time as different groups of Leeds arrived by train. The Ointment had loads out, despite many of the older lads being abroad. Small groups of Leeds were being picked off as they made their way from the

Interchange to the ground. The atmosphere in the city was tense and some Ointment members had come tooled up with blades, coshes and knuckle dusters. A group of Leeds fans were ambushed on Manningham Lane before the game. One, a 21 year-old plasterer, was slashed with a Stanley knife and needed 27 stitches down his back. The Service Crew got its act together at Valley Parade where all the lads from different parts of the country met up. It was probably the biggest mob ever to have come to Bradford up to then. The Ointment was on the back foot both inside and outside the stadium. Leeds brought 1,000 fans over for this game and half must have been lads. It was impressive. Numbers wise, the Service Crew was one of the top four mobs in England at this time. The Ointment was taught a lesson at Valley Parade and one it wouldn't forget.

Leeds United (H)
(Odsal)
09/04/86

Jimmy
THIS was a night match and I couldn't wait to finish work and get into town. I clocked off a bit early and was in The Queen by 5 pm. All the Ointment were meeting up Manchester Road, near Odsal Stadium, but I was waiting for a pal. While in the pub I recognised an old punk lad called Johna from the Bradford area. He was a Leeds fan but also a bit of a one off as a few of the older City lot liked him even though he travelled to matches with the Service Crew. One year the Ointment heading to Millwall spotted him waiting at a bus stop in London. They stopped and took him with them. But he wasn't well known to the Panel Beaters or Section 5, a group of younger lads attached to the Ointment. This fact would have serious consequences later.

I arrived at the Marshfields Pub, off Manchester Road and it was heaving with lads. There also, were two football intelligence officers in plain clothes. They tried to dress like hooligans to fit in but everyone knew who they were. Some of the lads used to have a laugh with them and after a while you got used to having them around. About an hour before the game we all set off towards Odsal. Up to this point nobody had seen Leeds anywhere. Then as we all headed up Bolingbrook Street, about 200 Service Crew came running around the corner at the top of the street. The numbers were pretty much equal but they had the advantage of the hill. As they got closer we were bombarded with rocks and they were bouncing all over the street as you jumped out of the way. The sky was full of missiles. The two football cops cleared off sharpish as Leeds got closer. To the side of us was a waste ground full of building materials and unknown to the Service Crew, another little mob of City had gathered getting stocked up with ammunition to throw back. I remember a weird silence when the rocks stopped coming. We were still on the road and had not backed off much. You could tell the Leeds lads didn't know what to do next. Suddenly they started getting bombarded from the left and there was a huge roar as we charged back up the street towards them armed with anything we could get hold of. They started to panic and back off before turning around and running like fuck. I've never seen as many lads run off before. It was an impressive sight in some ways. Some of them were jumping over garden fences and into houses. It was mass panic. Sadly, one lad who did not get away was Johna. He probably just came down with the Leeds lads for a look and didn't feel the need to run off. Unfortunately he was with the Leeds group and he got caught. He took a beating and was slashed down the back in the confusion. When some of the older lads realised what had happened they stayed with him until the ambulance arrived. Johna was, and still is, a popular lad in Bradford. He received 27 stitches but made a good recovery.

Meanwhile, at Bankfoot, the Service Crew had congregated behind a wall of police vans looking to be escorted to the stadium. Many Ointment members were pissed off about what had happened to Johna and there was a feeling of wanting to crack these cunts for leaving him. They had a giant of a lad with them known as China, or the Honey Monster. This bloke was massive. A few City lads managed to get around him. One of our lads called Murkey kicked him and China started having breathing problems and sweating. In all the confusion the police started marching us up to the ground together. It was fucking crazy as little fights were going on all over the place. Near Odsal, the escort erupted in violence with Leeds and City lads knocking fuck out of one another. Mounted police had to sort this out. When we got up to the ground some Leeds had paid into the stand meant for home supporters but they had lines of police around them. After the game City had hundreds down Manchester Road waiting for another crack at Leeds but the police were well on top of things.

Telegraph & Argus:
" A Leeds United fan needed 27 stitches after being kicked to the ground and beaten with a stick before the clash with Bradford City at Odsal. He suffered injuries to his head, arm and back after being dragged across broken glass. He was taken to Bradford Royal Infirmary where 27 stitches were needed. Seventeen arrests were made outside the stadium but no one else was injured."

Tragedy
12/06/86

Jimmy

I WAS in the Flagship Bar in the city centre when a lad called Chicken came in and said Huddersfield were in town. I was actually out on a lad called Taggy's birthday who happened to be a Leeds fan and one of their main faces. So we went outside and there was this scene of chaos with people running up and down the street and the sound of sirens in the distance. Taggy turned round to me and said: "These lads are Leeds, we're off back in the pub." About 50 Service Crew were outside the Rams Revenge. There were only a few Ointment lads about as it turned out loads were having it with black lads from Huddersfield in another part of town. I ran over and smacked this lad but got a plank of wood in my face. As this is all going on I spotted an original Ointment lad called Spike on the floor with a group of Leeds over him. What I didn't know until later was the bastards had used a blade on him. A few more City lads started to appear and the police had flooded the top of Ivegate trying to keep us and Leeds apart. Less than a quarter-of-a-mile away it's kicking off with Huddersfield big time too but at the time I knew nothing about it. I was in a weird spot as I had my nose spattered by Leeds but was also out boozing with some of them. I had to put my neck on the line and stopped the lads I was with getting a hiding. They were Leeds lads but they had played no part in the aggro and were not with the Service Crew who had come over on the train. My nose was all over my face and I could not stop the blood flowing. Leeds had fucked off back to the train station. So as things are calming down a bit I headed up to the Bradford Royal Infirmary to get it sorted. The emergency ward was packed with lads from Bradford,

172

Huddersfield and Leeds with the old bill trying to keep order. I noticed one lad who is well respected in Bradford, in tears on the corridor. He told me that Darrell had been stabbed and had died. That was the first time I even knew it had been going off with Huddersfield as well. I saw Spike and he was bandaged up across the face after being knifed by Leeds. Bradford city centre had become a war zone that warm summer's night. No one knew Leeds were coming and although there had been trouble with some of our young lads and Huddersfield in previous weeks, no one expected them to come over tooled up either.

Telegraph & Argus:
"More than 100 youths from soccer gangs Bradford City Ointment, Leeds Service Crew and Huddersfield Crew clashed for about two hours between 8 pm and 10 pm in flare-ups throughout the city centre. The Ointment's younger followers –the Bradford Section Five with members as young as 13 years-old were also involved. Det Supt Eric Thompson said: "Several of the youths were armed with numerous weapons and as a result of the stabbing we are looking for a particular knife. He said most of the weapons were Stanley type knives."

The following Saturday Taggy invited me to Leeds for a night out. I was unsure about it to be honest. These cunts had slashed Spike and it would only take one prick to get funny and I could be in trouble. But I went anyway. We goes into this pub called The Whip in the city centre and a good few of Leeds' top lads are in there. Pernod Harry, Dutton, Ward, Big Winston, Para Dave were a few I remember. I felt a bit uncomfortable but I stayed out with them anyway and to be fair I don't think I had to dip my hand in my pocket once. They knew a lot of names in Bradford and we were just having chats about this and that. They were even asking me to games and stuff. We went to all the Service Crew haunts such as Jackomellis and Harlequins before ending up in this warehouse type place. We were in there and I was told that Leeds lads had been having trouble with black lads from the Chapletown area and they had turned out for them. I went outside to have a look and Leeds had a right crew outside. A good 150 lads on a Saturday night out of season, fair play to them. But by the end of the night this Pernod Harry was becoming a pain in the arse so I fucked off back to Bradford.

Leeds United (H)
20/09/86
THE football authorities had lifted an all-ticket away restriction on Leeds fans which had been implemented as a result of trouble at away games. For whatever reason, the ban was lifted for this powder keg fixture and fans could now pay at the gate. Most of the Ointment were drinking at the Red Ginn in West Bowling. This pub was on the edge of a rough intimidating tower block estate known as Newby Square which is now demolished. It was about half-way between the city centre and Odsal Stadium. The Ointment knew if the Service Crew came by train, they would have to come in this direction to Odsal. Hanging around town would be a waste of time as the police would have been on top of things. Newby Square was a concrete jungle and a different matter altogether. Word had got around that Leeds had arrived about 10.30am. They had attacked a couple of pubs where the Ointment normally drank, smashing windows. There must have been 400 Ointment in and around Newby Square. The police had introduced the Hoolivan in West Yorkshire for this game and it spent all morning outside the Red Ginn. Basically it was a normal

police transit with a large revolving camera on the roof. Around 11.15 am about 150 Leeds were spotted walking up Manchester Road and the Ointment started sprinting through Newby towards them. Through the gaps in the maze of flats and tower blocks, many Leeds must have seen what was coming towards them. Two-thirds of them were off like a shot back towards town. Some stood by The Listers Pub and got dragged about a bit before the police arrived. These lads who had a go were from the Shipley/Bradford area. Shortly after, a convoy of three buses were escorted up Manchester Road with more of the Service Crew onboard. They could have got off with a little bit of effort but all they did was stick their fingers up and do wanking signals. It was a real shame as it could have been a real do at that point as most of our lads were there. Further up the road Leeds did get off the bus and it kicked off in subways, on roundabouts and in the middle of the dual carriageway. The police had lost control of the situation with battles raging all over the place. Two police officers took a savage beating from members of the Ointment which led to lengthy prison sentences being dished out.

Yorkshire Post:

"Serious trouble broke out before the match when two police officers were attacked by a mob of 60 youths stoning passers-by, traffic and nearby houses. Inspector Tom Lawrie, 46, drafted in from Keighley and Graham Hannam, 30, from Dudley Hill, Bradford, were beaten to the ground as the youths – white-West Indian and Asian- tried to stop them making arrests. The officers were kicked to the ground, hit with stones, and one was attacked with an iron bar and left unconscious. The attack was so violent that Insp Lawrie had to be given oxygen while he lay on the ground. PC Hannam was badly bruised and suffered a broken leg."

The Hoolivan was up and down grass embankments in Newby Square trying to get on top of things. It looked like an out of control Dalek. Inside Odsal, Leeds fans were congregated on the big open terrace along the side. Some had paid into the home seats but just huddled into a corner with dozens of police around them while City fans made repeated efforts to get at them. But an incident during the second-half is what this game is remembered for the most. Leeds supporters started shaking a fast food van on the steep embankment in the away section. The owner managed to escape as they turned it over. But in terrible scenes, it set on fire. Dark smoke bellowed into the air as traumatised City and Leeds supporters fled the ground. Some were in floods of tears. As the referee took the players off the pitch, Leeds fans climbed over the barriers and headed towards the home sections of the stadium. Some used the corner flags to launch into the fleeing home supporters. Hundreds of Leeds fans were on the pitch and scores tried to climb into the main stand where members of the Ointment had gathered. Fights broke out on the fence between rival supporters. But instead of clearing the Leeds fans off the pitch the police were forcing City fans out of the stand using truncheons. Meanwhile the fire brigade arrived to put the fire out but were forced back by Leeds fans pelting them with rocks. As this is going on the Hoolivan is driving around the perimeter track filming it.

Yorkshire Post:
"Shortly after Bradford City scored a group of Leeds fans started throwing missiles indiscriminately into lower terraces. Stones fell on other Leeds supporters including women and children, many of whom were treated for head injuries by medical staff. At least 10 people were taken to

hospital by ambulance although a spokesman said up to 20 had gone to hospital with various injuries."

The scene was one of utter chaos. Meanwhile outside the stadium, hundreds of Ointment had gathered near the Richard Dunn Sports Centre. It wasn't long before the Service Crew joined them and a mass brawl involving 400 lads took place on the adjoining cricket pitch. Fences were ripped to pieces and used as weapons as the two mobs clashed. Leeds eventually backed off with some running back into Odsal. But for the rest of the evening the Ointment would find itself overstretched fighting different mobs of up to 150 strong down Manchester Road. Lads from all over the country had come with Leeds this day and it was pure mental. Despite the Ointment having its biggest form ever, the battles with Leeds after the game was the equivalent of taking on four or five teams with decent firms at once. They were all over the place. Bradford had plenty of successes but you just have to hold your hands up and admit Leeds just had too many to cope with afterwards. On Manchester Road local West Indian youths and a small pocket of Asians had converged looking to get stuck into Leeds. In one part of West Bowling several crates of petrol bombs had been prepared. They were never used.

Chris
ONE thing that sticks in the mind about this game is Leeds had a few Cockney black lads with them. We had a row with them and we were surprised as you would associate Leeds with being racist at the time. From morning 'til night we were at it. I've never been involved in so many rows in one day.

In one fight we had I got hit by a car and I was a bit out of it. But this Leeds lad saw what happened and helped me up. I was in a daze and did not know where the fuck I was. There was fighting all over the place and people running about. It must have been near kick-off and me and this Leeds lad were walking up to the ground, fair play to him for helping me out. But as we got near the ground some Ointment lads appeared and when they found out this lad was Leeds they knocked fuck out of him. I was sorry about that but the atmosphere that day was pure nasty. He had a ticket for our end so he would probably have got a kicking anyway but I was sorry as he had helped me and picked me up from the floor. During the game Leeds fans were fucking about and turned a chip van over. Odsal had huge areas that were just like waste ground and this van rolled over and set on fire. Hundreds of Leeds fans spilled onto the pitch. The Bradford City Fire was still fresh in many City fan's memories and a lot of people just got out of the ground as soon as they spotted flames. The match got suspended and the pitch ended up full of Leeds. The Service Crew came across the pitch and made a run at the home stand. A lot of the Ointment had not even bothered going to the game but there was still a fair few about wanting to have a go at Leeds. As we got over the fence to meet Leeds the coppers started beating us back with truncheons. After the game we went up to Richard Dunn Sports Centre which is directly opposite Odsal. There were a good 200 City lads who had not gone to the game hanging about. We then spotted a right mob of Leeds heading our way. Easily 300. I turned round to Jimmy Cooper and said:

"We're fucked here."

Then I heard these snapping sounds. The Ointment lads had started pulling a fence apart to get sticks. So that was it. We were going to have a go. We ran down the hill and bang into them. Leeds didn't budge either so it was a good row until the old bill arrived.

Badger

WE all met in the Red Ginn and it was the first time the Hoolivan, basically a police van with a huge revolving camera, had been used in Yorkshire. The old bill and the government were at this time really coming down hard on lads involved in football violence. There were possibly 400 of us out that day. Some were not regulars but had come to have a pop at what was seen as the National Front mob. Leeds also had a huge turnout that day after an all-ticket away ban had been lifted. There was vermin from every part of the country. Before the match we had it with a load of Leeds on a football pitch up Manchester Road. It was a pitched battle for a few minutes until Leeds were on the retreat. They had black lads with them and I remember one of them with a Cockney accent calling a mixed race lad of ours who sadly passed away, Sean Durrant a "nigger". Others had southern accents, midlands accents, the lot. They even had lads from Sweden. It was then I knew we were up against something we had never faced before, a team with scores of separate mobs. Despite our very good numbers I knew we would eventually get stretched and that is what happened. We ended up smothered.

Paul Durrant

MOST of our lads met in the Red Ginn but about 80 of us met at the Yarn Spinners at the bottom of Manchester Road. There were some Traveller lads in there too who wanted to stick around with us for the day. We weren't complaining and one of them, Gervais, ended up coming about with us regularly. Sadly he is no longer with us. After watching the strippers we set off up the road to meet up with the rest of the lads. Loads of Leeds were making their way up as well. They were from all over the country and there wasn't a Yorkshire accent amongst this lot. The police dog handlers separated us but these Service Crew kids from Leicester way were giving me racist shit. The police told me to ignore it but I snapped and put one right on his arse. Straightaway I was lifted and put in the back of a van and the coppers gave me a good kicking. A Leeds fan in the van was telling them to leave me alone but they went well over the top on me. They drove me up to Odsal and put me in a mobile cell block and it was full of lads from both sides fighting. One of the main faces in Leeds at the time was a kid called Para Dave. We both served in the forces and we get along. I was eventually taken down to the Bridewell and the place was heaving with nicked lads. There were over 100 arrests. I remember this dozy Swedish cunt who made the headlines for being involved in the chip van fire. So I'm in this cell with another City lad and two Leeds fans including Para Dave. We agreed not to fight and ended up playing cards.

As time goes on everyone is getting out including the lads in the cell with me. Then at 4 am the door opened and the copper said detectives have applied for a 12 hour extension to keep me. They said it was for a serious assault on two police officers. What the fuck? I hadn't a clue what they were talking about and no one explained anything to me. Then in the early hours of Monday morning I start to hear shouting and voices in the cells next to me.

"Who's that? It's Chalky, who's that? It's John." And so on.

Loads of Bradford lads had been dawn raided and arrested for seriously beating up two police officers on Manchester Road. One was my brother Sean, who sadly passed away in 2009. I appeared in court on the Monday along with seven other Ointment lads. The judge ordered us to be remanded to the police cells until Thursday for further questioning. I thought I was being framed until I was called to a room for questioning. The CID told me they'd made a mistake and that I had already been arrested when the police had been beaten up so they knew I wasn't anything to do with it. But they said they couldn't let me go until the judge said it was OK. So I stayed in a cell in the police station with its door left open until Thursday. Even though they knew I had nothing to do with it. I was eventually bailed with conditions. I should have been released within minutes and my brother ended up on remand for six months and he had nothing to do with it either. He was eventually cleared. The whole thing was a legal joke.

Wild Thing

I MET Para Dave a year later in a police station in Leeds. I had been pulled in for questioning over something not football related .The police put me in a day cell alone and I fell asleep. But when I woke up I was far from lonely. I was amongst fourteen leading members of the Service Crew who had just been lifted as part of 'Operation Wild Boar'. This was an undercover investigation by police to try and bring an end to organised violence at Leeds matches in 1987. For fuck's sake! The first person to say anything was Para Dave who announced: "This is Durrant, he's one of the Ointment lads."

They all looked at me and I thought this could be interesting. But they were all sound and I guess they had other things to worry about. I eventually got moved to another cell and I was put in with a bloke called Joanna from Bradford. He was a well known transvestite who had been caught shoplifting. Joanna was brushing his hair as I walked in. I was more worried about him than the Service Crew lads. I never shut my eyes once.

Telegraph & Argus:
"A military style campaign to stage the "Battle of Bradford" at Odsal Stadium was drawn up by soccer yobs based in the

city, police believe. Detectives were today quizzing two fans who were at a meeting in the city centre six days before the game. The meeting was organised by leaders of the three gangs which have brought shame to the name of Bradford City. Detective Chief Inspector David Smith named the violent groups as – Ointment, The Panel Beaters and Section 5. The blueprint for riots included 'snatch squads' on police to release any gang members arrested. A number of officers were attacked when trying to make an arrest and a number of people have been remanded in custody. One officer is still in hospital with suspected lung damage. Det Chf Insp Smith said representatives of the three groups met in a city centre pub the Sunday before the match.

He said: " They formulated battle plans for the following Saturday and included was an agreement that if any of them were arrested, if the circumstances warranted, the police would be set on by the remainder of the group in an effort to release them."

The thugs also made plans for where they would meet to attack Leeds fans. Police are now considering conspiracy charges against the ringleaders, which carries a maximum sentence of life.

Leeds fan Tony H*****n, 20, knifed in the stomach during a fight in the city centre was today "satisfactory" in Bradford Royal Infirmary."

Leeds United (A)
01/01/88

Andy Hindle

SOMETHING like 39,000 were at this game with at least 8,000 City fans around the ground. Before the game a handful Leeds fans had got into the City seats looking for a go. This was funny in that they got twatted by regular supporters. They started off at the top of the seats and were being kicked and beaten by scarfers, old men and even children until they ended up in this shelf that separated the seats and the standing area like a no-man's land. Thousands of City fans were eagerly waiting for them below. They were absolutely shitting themselves until the police rescued them. Everyone in the ground was laughing at them as they were taken to safety.

Back To Basics

Dean

I WAS in Back to Basics in Leeds in about 1989, it was the height of the rave scene and people from all over would be at this club. This particular night there was only a few of us. But there had been sporadic trouble with the Service Crew and HYC lads from Huddersfield. We decided to leave and headed back to the train station. On the way we see these two sets of lads brawling in the street and we sort of knew we'd get dragged into it. I'm thinking like fucking hell what do we do here? So we just steamed in to the Leeds lot. The Huddersfield lads were by now cowering away and had bottled it. Leeds knew we weren't with them by this stage. We backed them off but we knew they would be back with more. We walked round the back of the train station and the Huddersfield lads had frozen to the spot. They daren't go round the corner. We were asking: "What's up with you? "

But they were useless. Leeds had come back now with a few more lads, one called Calverley Macca. He's asking:

"Who the fuck are you?"

But none of them are standing like they want a go. So I just smashed this cunt in the face and said:

"Bradford Ointment."

They scattered and we got in taxis and fucked off home before the old bill got involved. I looked out of the back window as we were leaving, to the left SC lads are stood and on the right Huddersfield. I think neither could believe what had just happened.

Leeds United (A)
Carling Cup
29/10/98

Phil
FIFTY of us left the Craven Heifer in taxis and arrived in Leeds about 5 pm. We got off near Spencers bar where we knew they would all be at. It was packed with their lads. One of ours banged on the window and they all started coming out. We were in the railway tunnel a few hundred metres away when the old bill wrapped us up. All of us got nicked and never made the game. There was loads of the cunts and with the small numbers we had it could well have come on top but we put it to them on their doorstep. Over 100 City fans got detained or nicked.

Leeds United (H)
12/03/00

Steff
ALL the pubs in the city centre were shut down for this game. One of our lads who had won the lottery owned a club at the time and he was told by the police he would be shut down if he opened before this game. Eventually we managed to get a licensed Indian restaurant to open for us. We had to reserve the place for a party so it was booked in the name of the Bradford Football Intelligence Officer at the time. Well over 300 were packed to the rafters in there.

A good mob of 200 Leeds had by-passed Bradford and met up in Shipley. They were hanging about outside pubs so it was no surprise they attracted the attention of the police. And it wasn't long before we had the old bill hanging about outside the Indian place. They were completely on top of things filming everyone and stuff. It was a real pisser as everyone was keen to have a crack at Leeds. During the game some Service Crew got in the home seats, sang a few songs, and claimed a result. It was just a very frustrating day all round.

Leeds United (A)
09/08/11

Steff
PRIOR to this game tension had been building up with Leeds. A few weeks before the game a mob of Ointment youth had gone through to Leeds and attacked Spencers bar near the train station while Service Crew lads were boozing inside. Everyone knew there was a big chance it was going to go off. We went through in taxis at about 2 pm and managed to get into Leeds unnoticed. In previous meetings the Service Crew had slagged us off for getting wrapped up by the old bill or getting into Leeds too late. They claimed they had three boozers full of lads waiting, etc, etc. This time there would be no excuses. We met in Walkabout in Leeds city centre. Some of the lads were on the phone to Leeds lads as soon as we arrived. They knew where we were but failed to show, so after an hour we went on a Walkabout ourselves. By this time there was a good 120 although more were in different boozers in the city centre. There were some real old boys in this mob and we knew it would take some shifting.

We walked through the city centre unopposed but as we

went past Becketts a mob of Leeds came at us from a side street. There were about 80 of them and we had older lads at the front as we were expecting a few hundred to have a go. A few of them came at us but they were soon on their toes and ran down the street from where they had appeared. By this time the old bill had sussed Bradford and came weighing in with truncheons. Just as this finished I spotted one of the main lads at Leeds, a lad called Taggy, stood on the corner. I went up to him and he said Leeds was all out and they knew what had just gone off. Another little firm of City had been collared and the cops put us in a pub called The Varsity. There was a good 200 altogether. We had been in Leeds for three hours and pretty much did what you have to do in this day and age. We took the piss in Leeds city centre for hours and had a pop at whatever came our way.

We were kept in the boozer until 7 pm and then a fleet of buses took us up to the ground. After the game Leeds were hanging about near the ground giving it the big one with scores of old bill on the scene. One of our lads steamed into about 40 of their older lot and ended up on his arse but there was no real chance of anything happening near the ground without it at least being on camera. They had their chance, they had good numbers out in Leeds earlier in the day but bottled it.

Phil

WE all went over in mini-buses and taxis from different parts of Bradford and arranged to meet in the Walkabout Bar in the city centre. It was a night game but 150 of us were in Leeds by 3 pm. We were in contact with their lads but they were trying to get us to go to Holbeck. In the past they have complained that we turn up late or out of the way. So this time we did all they asked so it was down to them to do the running about. After hanging around for an hour there was no sign of Leeds and some of the lads were getting impatient. So we decided to wander down to their main drinking holes near the train station. We quietly walked down Park Row until we got near Becketts Bar.

There was this big shout and they came streaming out of a side street, maybe 80 or so. They came over the railings throwing glasses and stuff but got quickly put on their arses and then ran off. It was a shame as there was hardly any police about. One of the Service Crew lads who I know rang me up saying how pissed off he was that we had taken liberties in their town centre. Altogether we probably had about 250 lads in Leeds in one group or another from mid-afternoon. Leeds can take big numbers away, especially down south where a lot of their lads come from. They take 400 lads to Man Utd. But at home, for a firm with a big rep, they are pretty poor. A lot of very good lads turned out who have not been for a while, but I'm not sure if they will be arsed going to Leeds again. It's always the same.

Chapter Nineteen

ALBA AGGRO

BRADFORD Has hosted two games with big teams from Scotland in recent years. The matches with Glasgow Rangers and Aberdeen have also resulted in violence on the streets. Indeed clashes with the Dons infamous mob, the Aberdeen Soccer Casuals (ASC,) had significant ramifications for the Ointment. Some members were given prison sentences and scores banned from attending football matches for long periods. For several years following Aberdeen, the Ointment was a relatively spent force with the police confident they had finally put an end to its activities. Many of the lads stopped going altogether and rival firms, who normally wouldn't show in Bradford, started taking liberties. This decline was only reversed with the emergence of the Young Bradford Ointment, who became the only active hooligan firm during this period.

The game with Rangers was supposed to be a friendly occasion as 10,000 supporters of the Scottish club descended on the Yorkshire city to pay tribute to Stuart McCall. However, police made 46 arrests as the Ointment and the Rangers Inter City Firm battled it out on the streets.

Afterwards, one of the top boys in the ICF, Davey Carrick, in his book, ICF Rangers, described Bradford as having one of the top firms in England. He revealed fighting the Ointment was one of the best battles he's ever been involved in.

Aberdeen (H)
26/07/03

Mark
ABERDEEN brought 150 lads down for this pre-season friendly and had been picking off scarfers before the match. They had been staying in Leeds the night before and had Spurs lads with them too. It had gone off a bit on Manningham Lane and a few got arrested. After the match we were in the Goose pub when we got a message saying Aberdeen were coming through the city centre. We walked up Ivegate and they came running round the corner at us. It's a really steep hill and they had the advantage of more numbers and the hill. But when they realised we weren't budging, their arses went. We kicked fuck out of them and you can see that on YouTube. The police were there pretty quick though and they sealed Ivegate off so the Ointment lads couldn't get away. Everyone got their photo taken before being let go. A while later I got dawn raided during Operation Olive. Twenty doors got kicked down that morning. I went "No comment" for 24 hours. The police were saying they were going to check CCTV and get me through facial mapping. But I eventually got identified by a bird I've never seen before and charged. I got sent to jail for four months and a six year ban in 2003. There are cameras everywhere now and you cannot get away with anything. Eight lads from Bradford got prison for this.

Telegraph & Argus:
"Eight Bradford men have been jailed for their part in clashes with visiting football fans in Bradford city centre.

They were also banned from all football matches for periods ranging from six to seven years, as the police and Crown Prosecution Service sought a new crackdown on football-related violence.

The city's magistrates court heard how punches and kicks were exchanged when Bradford City fans clashed with Aberdeen supporters in Ivegate on July 26. The match was part of City's Centenary Tournament.

More than 100 hooligans were involved in the violence on Ivegate on the afternoon of Saturday, July 26, the first day of the tournament, which was billed as a family event.

Bottles and hoardings were thrown and a police dog was injured when the windscreen of a police van was smashed as officers restored order.

Twelve people were arrested on the day and a further nine arrests were made after more than 20 hooligans from the two clubs brawled in Manningham Lane on the same afternoon.

Sentencing some of those involved yesterday District Judge David Thomas said the incident - which lasted only 37 seconds - blighted the city which had suffered from riots in July 2001.

He said: "Bradford has had its share of problems in the last few years and, while this was not like the events of 2001, incidents of this nature bring discredit on the city.

"This was a serious city centre incident, fortunately nipped in the bud by the prompt action of the police. The citizens of Bradford were entitled to walk the streets in safety without having to face such incidents perpetrated by "supposed football supporters" who were really "hooligans", he added.

Chief Inspector David Lunn, in charge of the operation, said police would not accept the serious organised violence that took place in Ivegate.

He said: "Our message is that Bradford City Football Club and West Yorkshire Police will not tolerate such behaviour. It is unacceptable. At the end of the day people have died through football violence. It must stop now."

Chief Insp Lunn said violence had moved away from the grounds to city centres, with a knock-on effect for other people.

He added: "We want Bradford to be a safer place for people to come to and we won't allow football hooligans to disrupt people going about their business."

Seven Aberdeen fans have been identified after West Yorkshire Police sent posters of suspects to Scotland."

Glasgow Rangers (H)
29/04/02

RANGERS fans drinking in The Queen bar before the match got talking to some Ointment members before the game. They were persuaded to head further into town and assured they wouldn't get any trouble. They agreed and made their way to Ivegate. However, they walked straight into an ambush. Over 80 Ointment attacked them from a side street forcing the Rangers fans to scatter in all directions. A number were badly beaten. After the match around 150 members of the Rangers ICF clashed with the Ointment on waste ground less than a mile from Valley Parade. Hand-to-hand fighting took place for over five minutes as both groups refused to budge. Police intelligence officers who had followed the ICF filmed the whole incident.

Steff
THIS was Stuart McCall's Testimonial match and Rangers brought 10,000 supporters down for it. I got a phone call

leading up to the game by one of the top boys in the Rangers Inter City Firm saying they were bringing a mob down. I knew that the Ointment were up for it as well. It was an awkward situation for me so I kept out of it. Some Rangers lads came by train and others had gone to Blackpool by coach. Loads of Rangers fans travelled from other parts of England too. None of us had gone into the match but we knew Rangers had brought a crew. I wasn't involved in anything before the game. After the match we were all in an old West Indian club near Valley Parade. Somebody came in and said they are here. As we got out, hundreds of Rangers were on us. We were all over the place and they had us on our toes. But we all got together in the city centre and we clashed with them again at the top of Ivegate. This time Bradford had them.

Bradford Ointment coming up the street as Aberdeen and Yids back off in 2003.

Due to a serious disorder
at a licenced premises
in Bradford City Centre,
the persons named below
have been given
a life-time ban from
City Centre Public Houses

Anthony Ali
Born 20-10-81

Luke Greaves
Born 4-9-84

Daniel Wright
Born 23-8-84

Chapter Twenty
YOUNG BRADFORD OINTMENT

AFTER Aberdeen, with bans and the prison sentences dished out, the Ointment was at its weakest. Teams such as Wigan were coming to Bradford and doing as they pleased. Nobody seemed to be bothered anymore. The demise of organised football violence in the city seemed to be inevitable. However the emergence of a younger gang of hooligans began to gain itself notoriety in the city. They travelled independently to away games and forged a reputation for causing havoc in the lower leagues. This group has since become one of the most active youth firms in the country.

They are known as the Young Bradford Ointment (YBO). Its original leader was Danny Wright (27). He is currently banned from football until 2016 and when he next steps foot inside Valley Parade he will have been banished from the stadium for a total of 13 years. As recently as July 2012 Danny was forced to hand over his passport by West Yorkshire Police who feared he may travel abroad to follow City in a pre-season match.

The YBO has now itself got its own youth wing, the Under Five's, who have been responsible for attacking the Service Crew in a Leeds city centre bar, and stoning away fans and their coaches in recent times. Here Danny gives a frank account of his time with YBO and reveals some of the shocking acts of violence he was involved with. He tells how an infamous appearance on the TV show 'Real Football Factories' was used against him in a high profile court case. And how police footage of a brawl involving the YBO and Rotherham fans is now splashed across a must have clothing range called 'Weekend Offender'.

Danny does not try and make out he was anything other than a football hooligan. He does not try to glamorise his activities. His lengthy spell in jail, fines and banning orders should act as a deterrent to any teenager thinking of becoming involved.

DANNY

THE first real taste of football violence I experienced was in January 2003 when City had played away at Rotherham. Eighty of us went by service train and it was a mix of old and young lads. As usual at places like Rotherham, we just took the piss and the whole day in South Yorkshire was pretty much a non-event. But we were all looking forward to going back home as we had to change trains in Leeds, and we knew they would be waiting for us. We arrived about 6.30 pm and Leeds had been playing West Brom at home that day. As we are pulling in we spotted a decent mob of Leeds on the platform and more coming down the steps. They were giving it large as the train slowly pulled in but you could see in their faces they were not expecting quite so many of us to turn up. We all got off and went straight in. They didn't even stand to have a go. They were on their toes straight away. We ran them back up the steps that crossed the railway lines and at the other end they were jumping over the barriers to get away. One of them turned around and was smacked and tumbled down some escalators. It was funny to watch. About fifteen of us got through the barriers and chased them through the station into the city centre. But by this time some of those who bottled it had gone to get more Service Crew from the Scarborough Taps pub. Loads of them started bouncing over and it went off. Lot of screaming "Ointment Mental" and that sort of thing. The police came and separated it and were getting stuck in with their truncheons. One of our lads pulled one off the copper and he started spraying pepper spray around. It got a few of the lads right in the face. During the fighting a disabled man fell off his wheelchair and this was reported in the newspapers. The Service Crew took great delight on football forums blaming us for it. A convenient distraction for them getting run. Leeds had been playing West Brom that day and some of their lads in the train station witnessed it all.

Sheffield Wednesday (H)
18/03/03

THIS was a night game and about 30 of us, a mix of Ointment and YBO, did not bother going to the game and went for a drink on Manningham Lane. At the away game a decent mob went to Sheffield but was turned back from getting in to the city by the police. We waited for Wednesday to come out after the match and we spotted a mob of their lads, known as the Owls Crime Squad (OCS), outside the Bradford Arms. The good thing about this was the YBO could see them but they had no idea the YBO were coming. It was a good buzz the build up to this as these cunts were going to get a big shock. As we got to the pub a roar was let out and the OCS were panicking. A Polish lad of ours kicked it off by smashing a kid in the face with a traffic cone and it was a good little off. A few of them had a go but fled back in the pub with one silly cunt defending himself with the cushion side of a stool. He ended up battered. The YBO steamed into the bar and Wednesday were throwing what seemed like the whole pub out. Within a few minutes the police helicopter was hovering above and the old bill were running towards the bar. A few got arrested for this later.

Aberdeen (H)
26/07 /03

I WAS 18 years-old at the time of this game and was already hooked on the whole football scene. Not just the violence but the clothes, the camaraderie, the nights out. Everything about it appealed to me. The game with Aberdeen took place during a tournament to celebrate Bradford City's centenary and was a 1.45 pm kick-off on a Sunday. There had been rumours the Aberdeen Soccer Casuals (ASC) would come and they did, a good 150 of them. They have a thing going with Spurs too, when they play in England they team up with the Yids. So there were a few of them tagging along as well. First time I clocked them was outside the Bradford Arms pub on Manningham Lane. We had no idea where they were and this was by chance. It was still early in the day. Most of our lads had gone on Lumb Lane, which runs parallel. We had a decent set of lads out, a good 80-100. The ASC were different from other mobs I've seen. They were mostly dressed well but they were also rowdy and fucking loud. Singing and shit like that. A few of us walked past and there were only a couple of community policemen with them at this time. Anyway this div in a Reebok Classic t-shirt shouts over: "Where's your mob?" I told him not to worry he'd know soon enough. The silly twat then threw a pint glass at me. Just as this happens a few of the Ointment came down the side of the pub and Aberdeen start getting ready. One of their main lads, a big cunt, starts talking to a kid called Macca who proceeds to spark him. It all kicks-off then and I'm at it with this big bald fella.   We held our own but if more police had not arrived almost straight away then we would have got a good kicking.

After the game it really kicked off when the Ointment and the ASC clashed in the city centre. Obviously I missed it but you can see what happened on YouTube. The Ointment kicked fuck out of them, it's there for everyone to see.

A good few ended up getting jail and loads more had their doors kicked down early in the morning. My co-accused was the lad I was fighting with. When we were in court eight months later he turned up with the lad who Macca chinned. He could not speak properly. His jaw was still wired up with the smack he got outside the Bradford Arms. They were alright these lads. The ASC has a good name throughout Europe and is regarded by many as the top mob in Scotland. But these lads said Bradford was the only place in England where they have come unstuck. They could not believe how rough a city it was. They told us Aberdeen still argue with each other about what happened in Bradford. It was their firm that got done. No excuses, they had loads. I got a ban and fined for this incident.

In 2004 the YBO started to get going. City was in League One at the time and there would be up to forty of us who regularly went to home and away games. We were having rows with the likes of Crewe, Chesterfield, Brentford, teams like that.

Chesterfield
28/08/04
ME and this lad called Shak went in the game near the end to see if Chesterfield had brought anything. I noticed about 10 lads in front but thought they must be ours as it was in the home seats. Anyway they jumped up and I jumped up

too because I thought City had scored. My mate then asked: "What you doing? Chesterfield has just scored." So one of ours banged this big cunt and he did not move an inch. He was fucking huge. We had a little do with them and then the stewards came and we went outside to continue it. This time the big cunt smashed me in the face and sent my flying over a car. When the game finished more and more City lads had turned up. Fair play to these lads from Chesterfield for having a go but they were outnumbered big time and fucked off in the end.

Brentford (A)
20/11/04

WE had arranged to go down there on mini-buses but the old bill had heard about our plans and talked the rental company into not giving us any transport. So at the last minute we decided to go by train. We got there early and had been drinking in boozers near the ground. At Griffin Park there is a pub on each corner of the ground. One of them was full of Celtic fans all wearing the shirts. We had no bother with anyone until one of ours was pulled near the ground by a West Ham lad wanting to know if we wanted a do after the game. West Ham was playing Millwall the following day. So they exchanged numbers and it was arranged we'd go to this wine bar after the match. About 20 of us went there after the final whistle and this West Ham kid was ringing up saying they'd be there in five minutes.

After more than an hour no one showed so we fucked off and headed for the Tube Station. But as we were walking along we heard this massive roar behind us. Fuck me, about 80-100 lads are on us. My mate Gracey gets put to the ground and I got knocked over the bonnet of a car by this ginger cunt. To be honest we were on our toes. I ended up sprinting up this road and jumped into this shop. I picked up two bottles of milk and pretended to be looking to buy an ice-cream from the freezer. As I'm doing this all these lads are running past shouting: "Where is the fat cunt?" When they went past I jumped in a taxi. I was lucky. We all met up and a few of ours had taken a beating. I found out later that the lads who had done us had in fact been to a BNP meeting in the area and included West Ham, Chelsea, Walsall, Aston Villa and Brentford lads.

Brentford (H)
16/04/05
WE carried on speaking to Brentford after what happened down there and we had arranged to meet them at Frizinghall Train Station after they changed at Leeds. This would mean them bypassing Bradford city centre. Everyone was up for giving them it and some of the YBO were tooled up with hammers and stuff. We were in contact with Brentford Youth from the moment they left London and fully expected them to show. They were due to arrive at midday but were not on the train. It turned out they had second thoughts and went for a drink in Leeds instead. About 25 of the YBO thought fuck this and decided to head over to Leeds looking for them. I'd also got a call from a Service Crew lad who told me he had seen Brentford in Leeds and they were acting the big misters. The YBO headed over to Leeds and met this Service kid who showed us which pub Brentford had set up in but they had fucked off. We eventually got to have a look at Brentford in Valley Parade later that day.

They had unveiled a BNP flag and were a bit of a shit outfit to be honest. Time wasters. I'm not saying the YBO were the largest firm in the world or whatever, but we always went looking for it, not like these jokers.

Swansea (A)
14/02/ 06

IT was a night game and twenty five of us had set off in rented cars at six in the morning from Bradford. We got to Swansea about midday and checked into a hotel. We were having a look round and I noticed this postman was staring at us. If you are involved in fighting at football you sort of know if someone is a lad too. It's hard to explain but you just know. I had this feeling about the postman. Anyhow I went back in the hotel and came back out again about 15 minutes later, and this postman is sat in his van just outside. So I went over to him and asked him if he was Swansea. He said he was and we exchanged numbers and he told me about a pub we should go to. We got sorted at the hotel and headed off to this pub. We were in having a pint and this big cunt dressed all in black walks in. He looked like a bouncer. He came over and asked who Danny was? So I stood up. He walks over and says give them an hour and they'll be back with a mob. We waited and they never showed but the old bill did! Anyhow five of us were banned so at about 6 pm we have to move five miles away from the ground. We end up in this place called Mumbles. It's like a mini-Blackpool which was a surprise because I had no idea Swansea was near the sea. We boozed there until our ban had finished and headed back into Swansea city centre at 11 pm. City drew the game 1-1. We were in Yates's having a drink and one of our lot chinned a kid. So we got thrown out of there and by this time there are about 18 of us. As we get outside, a mob of Swansea appear and it was straight in at one another. They had an old cunt at the front with a goatee beard that was game as fuck. But when he went down the others lost the appetite for it and backed off. Swansea had a bit of a reputation at this time. They are known as the Swansea Jacks and could pull decent numbers.

A big mob of theirs had gone into Manchester after they had played Bury the season before and done well by all accounts. Even though it was not big scale for the YBO to go down there, have a little show, and give them it in their own backyard without any of the Ointment lads, felt good.

Huddersfield (H)
7/10/06

THE two previous times we had played Huddersfield all of our older lads had turned out for this lot both home and away and got nothing. The best mob I've seen City have was for an away game with Huddersfield in 2004. A good 200 plus went that day with loads of old lads on it. We would have destroyed most mobs that day but Town were nowhere to be seen. When I was in jail in 2008, 150 Ointment were in Huddersfield from 3 pm for a night game. They only ever turn out for us when they know when no one is turning out. Lads from other clubs rate Huddersfield. I don't get it. So when we had played them this season it was really only the YBO who turned out in any numbers.

It was a 12 o'clock kick-off. One of our lads knew one of their lot and they said they would definitely turn out this time. We met in the Old Vic pub off Manchester Road at 9 am. They started ringing up about 10.30 am saying they were in Bradford and that we would find them if we looked. They were playing a stupid game of cat-and-mouse, but by chance we found out they were less than five minutes away at the Mill Lane Club. The YBO set off, a good 50, and by this time a few older lads were with us too. We had no fear about what was waiting. One of the lads went ahead in a car to tell Huddersfield to come out and we'd be there in minutes. They never came out so by the time I arrived a circle of City lads had formed at the door and glasses were flying and stuff. The YBO managed to push its way in and Huddersfield had a good mob in the club, all ages and sizes. I got attacked with snooker cues, beer bottles and pool balls. But they would not leave. As I stood by the door this bottle came flying through the air, over everyone's head, out of the door and smashed into this jeep. It was like special effects on the Matrix or something. Anyway someone shouted the coppers were here and everyone ran over Manchester Road. But there was no police and the Town lads had now come out of the club. The YBO went back over at them and not one of the Huddersfield lads stood. They ran straight back into the club and bolted the door behind them. Most of the YBO cleared off at this point but stupidly about ten went to another pub down the road. Half-an-hour later the Town lads copped for this ten and had them on their toes. Huddersfield claimed this as a result.

At the end of this season the YBO were in Halifax and we came across the Huddersfield Young Casuals (HYC). There were 20 of us and the same number of them. Their main lad is called Jay. He came up to me and was trying to be friendly and stuff. Fuck that. We steamed in, within minutes they were on their arses or running off. I'll give this Jay lad some credit as he stood but ended up getting a beating. They made excuses that they did not have their main lads with them, etc.

Blackpool (A)
28/10/06
THE year before, the Ointment took a right mob over to Blackpool on a Bank Holiday weekend. Two hundred had gone and fucked them all over. So we had a pretty good idea Blackpool would try and get a bit of revenge this time. About 30 of YBO went to Blackpool in vans and got there

about 9am. We later got in Wetherspoons and Blackpool sussed us out. Their firm are known as the "Muckers". They were telling us to head to this other boozer. Well after what Ointment had done the year before, chased them out of their own bars, there was a good chance they would have a decent firm waiting. I knew they were no mugs. They had recently turned Forest over.

So we stayed where we were. The onus was on Blackpool. A few of us were on bans which meant we had to get five miles away from the football ground at 1pm. So when we fucked off the lads left got impatient and thought fuck it, and ended up going to this pub where Blackpool were. They got there and were confronted with a right site. It was like B&Q had been emptied as the cunts piled out of this pub with spades, garden forks, pick axe handles, the lot. So it came on top and the YBO were on their toes. Some ended up in a builder's yard and were pelting rocks at Blackpool to keep the bastards at bay. The old bill arrived eventually and some of ours had taken a nasty beating. One lad was put in hospital. We were in Lytham St Annes while all this is going on and stayed there until 6 pm, when our bans were up. The YBO decided to go back into Blackpool in taxis but could only find two that would take us. So we set off and arranged to meet up again in a pub called the Princess Hotel. We walk in and we heard this: "They're over there." Blackpool are in the bar. Straight away it kicks off and it spills onto the street. It's about ten on ten at this point. I knew something was not right as they kept on backing off and trying to get us up this side street away from the bar. As we got to the corner there was this roar: "Sea-Sea-Seasiders." About 50 of the cunts come charging down this road so we fuck off back inside the bar. One of our lads got caught at the door and we were pulling him in as they were trying to get him out. He was shouting: "Don't let me go." Luckily we won this tug-of-war. One of the Muckers got in and he got a beating. But some of the YBO at the door were getting hit on the back of the head with ashtrays and glasses being thrown by other City lads behind them. Then I heard: "They've come in the fucking back door."

About 20 of them had got in and it went off. One City lad is using the karaoke microphone and whipping the bastards while another has this tray of dirty glasses and firing them off like a machine gun as more and more Blackpool pile in.

By this time another taxi had arrived with some of ours inside. But instead of fucking helping they got bags of chips and stood watching it. To be honest I thought we were going to get killed. For ten minutes we fought the cunts off but they kept on coming from one door to another. I mean ten minutes, not 30 seconds that seemed liked ten minutes. It seemed like three hours. They could sense blood. When the police arrived the pub looked like downtown Basra.

Everything was smashed to bits. All the staff had hid upstairs and were in shock. We were all knackered. The rest of the lads were turning up by now and police videoed us all and escorted us back to the vans. For pure violence this was the worst I have ever seen it for anything surrounding football.

The violent clashes made headlines in the local newspaper:

"AROUND 80 football hooligans clashed in Blackpool town centre on Saturday night.

The thugs were involved in pitched battles around the Chapel Street area following Blackpool's 4 -1 win over Bradford at Bloomfield Road.

Police were confronted by rowdy fans before the game and fighting continued after the final whistle in the streets surrounding the ground.

The Princess Hotel on Foxhall Road had windows smashed as the violence continued.

Police recommended the Royal Oak on Lytham Road close its doors after the match.

Manager Sarah Bettney said: "The police said to us there had been one or two incidents, although none of the fans drinking in our pub had been involved.

But because we do get a lot of football fans in on match days the police came in and said it might be a good idea to close because of the trouble which had already gone on.

We closed the doors from around 4.40pm and opened them back up at 6pm and we just let home fans in.

We didn't stop serving at any time, just closed the doors as a precaution.

Evidence gathering teams were out at the scene until late on Saturday and police have said they are confident of making arrests in the near future."

Oldham
18/11/06

WE were playing this lot at their place and a few calls had been made in the run up to the game. We decided to give Oldham a miss altogether and arranged to meet them in Rochdale instead. Fair play to Oldham, they are useless but they always turn up. We set off with only about 20 YBO and to be honest I thought we could end up getting a bit of a hiding. I knew Oldham could pull a lot more than that if they brought their full firm down. We got there on the train and went in this pub and the phone rang. Oldham were 100 yards down the road in another pub and thank fuck they had similar numbers out. You have to understand at the time the fights between youth mobs were small scale number wise. A lot of clubs had a youth firm who did their own thing like the YBO. So the plan was hatched with Oldham to head down an alleyway near both pubs and have it away from the cameras. It was a proper buzz to be honest heading down this alley. As soon as the YBO arrived we were pelted with bricks and bottles. One of theirs was actually a kid called Mickey from Stockport who later ended up getting six-years jail for football violence. He ended up on his arse and got a beating. The rest ran off and left him. Poor cunt. For the return fixture in April 2009, the YBO arranged to meet Oldham again. This time in Halifax. Same result.

Rotherham
December 2007 (game called off)
THE night before this game I was playing poker and had not got to bed until 6am. I was not expecting anything as Rotherham never brought anything to Bradford and were useless at home. They call themselves the Leather Jacket Crew. So I'm in bed when the phone rang about 11.30 am. A mate told me a coach full of Rotherham lads had been boozing on Huddersfield Road and were heading to Wibsey. This part of Bradford is where a lot of the Ointment would go drinking on a weekend and Rotherham knew where they were heading. The game had been called off because of the bad weather.

So I get up and get a few lads together and we head up to the Windmill Pub where they all are. A few of the YBO are hanging around outside and I think fuck this I'm off in. I walked into the bar and there is about 40 Rotherham in there. The City lads start hitting the cunts and one of ours smashed a good few over the head with a cosh. About nine YBO are with me. As the fighting gets more intense the Leather Jacket Crew are dragging me further into the pub.

My mates were pulling me back and eventually the sheer weight of numbers forced us out of the door and outside onto the street. I had taken a few smacks and was pissed off. Because of this I did not notice the police car over the road. Rotherham started to come out of the Windmill. I ran back and fired straight into them and they've ran back into the pub. It was then I spotted the police filming, I knew I'd fucked it. I knew I would get pulled in for this. Rotherham came out again and there was a bit of a stand-off but that was it. Rotherham were shit. Only ten out of a coach full came out.

Danny was indeed arrested five months later and convicted of affray in August 2008. He was jailed for 27 months for the offence and he believes he was made a scapegoat. "All the Rotherham fans arrested had their charges dropped" he said.

"And when I appeared in court they played a recording of me on Danny Dyer's 'Real Football Factories' talking about my links with the Ointment. The Judge did not like it."

His appearance on the cult football violence show has since been followed by police footage of the YBO's attack on the Rotherham mob, and Danny's leading role in it, becoming a major hit on YouTube.

Fists fly as mind-bending dance music beats to every punch thrown. The following is how the Bradford Telegraph & Argus reported Danny's court appearance:

"During an interview on The Real Football Factory, Bradford City follower Daniel Wright claimed clashes with rival supporters were "the best buzz in the world".

But a judge told him yesterday that his offending brought disrepute to the city and the club. Judge Jonathan Durham Hall QC heard that Wright was a member of the notorious Ointment gang and had twice been made the subject of football banning orders.

Prosecutor Louise Azmi told Bradford Crown Court that

the 24 year-old was still under a four-year banning order when he was involved in a confrontation with Rotherham United fans last December.

She told the court how the fixture with Bradford City had been called off because of bad weather, but some Rotherham fans ended up drinking at the Windmill Inn in Wibsey, Bradford. Judge Durham Hall watched police video footage of Wright throwing punches at rival fans in the doorway of the pub as fighting spilled out along the street.

Wright, who was not arrested until April, pleaded guilty to a charge of affray, and Mrs Azmi outlined details of his previous convictions which included football-related offences in March, 2004, and October, 2005.

The judge was also shown clips from the documentary programme in which Wright told the interviewer: "When it kicks off it's the best buzz in the world." As part of his sentence yesterday Judge Durham Hall imposed a new eight-year football banning order on Wright even though his barrister pointed out that its terms would not have prevented the incident in Wibsey.

The new order means that Wright, of Holmewood, Bradford, cannot go within a mile of Bradford City's ground on match days for three hours before the kick-off and two hours after the game has finished.

He faces a similar restriction on going to either of City's railway stations when City are at home and if they have an away game he must not go within five miles of an opponent's ground.

Wright's barrister Nigel Hamilton conceded that the latest incident was a serious one, but he pointed out that it was short-lived and his client had only used his fists during the fighting.

"While I accept that it is unpleasant and unlawful

violence…for this type of violence it is at the lower end of the scale," he submitted.

But Judge Durham Hall told Wright he was "a committed football hooligan" adding: "You clearly couldn't care less. You revel in your notoriety even finding some satisfaction in being part of a group childishly named the Ointment – a choice which indicates the intellectual level of this activity."

The judge said he intended to send out a message to others that the courts would not tolerate such offending."

I spent the first eight weeks in Armley, then Lindholme and finally the punishment jail Moorland, which was a fucking dump. Everything about it was horrific. They claimed I was planning to escape from Lindholme which was a load of shite. There were not many football lads. One was from Rotherham but he was in for drug dealing. We talked about a previous time when he'd been to Bradford and had all the windows of his mini-bus put through despite getting a helicopter escort to the motorway. Another was a Chelsea lad who was labelled Britain's Biggest Fraudster who was sound. A Derby County fella in for importing cocaine was a really good lad. He remembered the 80's when it used to kick off between us and them. Prison takes some getting used to but you get on with it. I'm banned for life from pubs in town, banned from football. I just get used to it.

Rochdale
19/01/ 08

SIX month before this game a few of our lot had been involved in a fight with Bolton lads at Manchester Victoria Train Station. It was supposed to have been a good do and some of the lads who got arrested swapped numbers. We later found out that Bolton are going to show at this fixture and team up with Rochdale. We met in the Interchange and to be honest I was surprised at the turnout. There was a good 150. A lot of older lads and YBO. We got the train and got to Rochdale about 11.30 am but by this time the game had been called off because of the weather. We ended up walking about but there was nothing doing so we ended up in this pub. It wasn't long before the West Yorkshire Police Football Intelligence spotters arrived outside. But because the game was off, those on a ban asked if they could stick around. We were thinking of heading to Manchester, but the police did not like that idea and told us to stay in Rochdale and we would not be breaking our ban. So we all went to Yates's Bar. One of our lads went for a wander to see if Bolton and Rochdale had surfaced and he was gone for ages. We eventually found them in a pub on the edge of the town. Everyone set off walking up this hill. By this time there was over 200 of us as some on the train who were not with us decided to tag on after the game was postponed. It was an impressive sight. An amazing sight.

We get near to this pub called the Bricklayers Arms and were marching up towards it when the Manchester Task Force Police pulled up in vans. They were straight into us, no messing. They were smashing us over the heads with metal truncheons. By this time Bolton and Rochdale had come out of the back of this pub and came for a go. A few got crumpled on the floor. But the police just kept on smashing people left-right-and -centre. They had no interest in arresting anyone as far as I could see. It was like they were in a riot situation with the policeman at the front screaming: "hold, hold" as they head towards us in a line. And more and more kept on pulling up. They eventually had us all round up. We fucked off and took over Halifax for the day.

Facebook
25/07/ 09

ONE of our lads had a problem in Bingley and his windows had been put through. Stuff had been said on Facebook too that had angered the YBO and some of the lads wanted a word with a bouncer working at the Foundry Hill pub. So about thirty went through along with a few older lads. It kicked off and windows got put through and people were jumping behind the bar. There is not much more I can add to what was reported in the Telegraph & Argus newspaper:

"A gang of six drunken hooligans who went on the rampage at a Bingley bar after a football match were today jailed for a total of more than ten years.

The thugs – one a self-confessed member of the notorious Ointment gang which follows Bradford City – stormed the Foundry Hill Bar in Bingley, following a match between City and Barnsley.

They were seeking revenge against a doorman at the bar who had posted "derogatory" messages on social networking site Facebook, Bradford Crown Court heard.

Terrified customers, including a pregnant woman, fled to the back end of the bar as the men poured in the front door at 8.15pm on July 25 last year.

Tom Leach, 21, Paul Clifford, 51, Kevin Butterick, 46, Gary Partridge, 39, and two 17-year-old youths have now been jailed after admitting violent disorder on July 25 last year.

Prosecutor Patrizia Doherty said they had been among a gang of between 20 and 30 men heading towards the bar, some chanting threats to "kill" the doorman, Samuel MacGregor.

Along with colleagues, he tried to shut the men out but – after smashing windows and a door – they barged through.

Mrs Doherty showed Judge Jonathan Durham Hall QC footage taken by the bar's CCTV of the men running into the bar and smashing chairs. The gang "trashed" the pub, causing £7,000 worth of damage, the court heard.

Judge Durham Hall said: "Inside that public house were perfectly normal, law-abiding, well-behaved members of the public, among them a pregnant lady. The distress is unimaginable."

Clifford, of Littlemoor Crescent,Pudsey, Leeds, admitted to police he was a member of Bradford's notorious Ointment hooligan firm but said he could remember little of the incident.

Butterick, of Buttershaw Drive, Bradford, also told police he had been too drunk to remember anything.

Partridge, of School Lane, Wibsey, and Leach, of Cooper Lane, Bradford, answered "no comment" in interview.

At yesterday's hearing, Leach was sentenced to 21 months for his part in the violence, with Clifford and Butterick receiving two-year sentences.

Partridge, who was previously jailed for violent disorder, was jailed for two and a half years.

The two 17-year-olds, who cannot be named for legal reasons, were given sentences of 12 and 18 months in youth detention centres.

All were given football banning orders for six years.
Judge Jonathan Durham Hall, QC, said: "This city is not alone in its experience of what happens when mobs go on the rampage. But this city has been scarred and its judges will not hesitate, in the face of mob violence, to move swiftly and robustly to punish you and deter others."

Chief Inspector Mick Hanks, of Airedale and North Bradford Police, said: "We welcome the decision of the courts today which sends a clear message that this kind of violent and anti social behaviour will not be tolerated."

Port Vale
15/08/09

I HAD only been out of jail a few weeks when I get a phone call saying a mob of Port Vale are in a small town near Bradford called Cleckheaton. Not many were interested so a car full of us drove up to have a look. We get there and spotted 15 of them outside this pub. We drive into a supermarket car park and as we are getting out I tell the driver to park the car facing out in case it comes on top. We start walking towards these Vale lads and they all start banging on the pub windows shouting: "they're here". We were fucked as another 35 or so come piling out. They come at us and we are backing off into the car park making our way back to the car. We are fighting for our lives. They seemed a little reluctant and I suspect they thought a load more City were about somewhere, thank fuck. Meanwhile, the driver had picked the worst possible position to park the car and was doing all these manoeuvres trying to get out of the parking spot as these Vale cunts are looking for blood. They now know our car and as we get to it they start kicking fuck out of it as we try to get in. About 10 Vale were concentrating on one of my mates and he had no choice but to back off. Some of them went after him but this do-gooder must have thought he'd nicked something with all these lads chasing him. So he grabs the YBO lad and the Vale lot catch up and pounce on him. By this time we managed to escape with the car kicked to fuck. The lad who got collared was lucky. He had a hole in his jacket where it looked like he had been stabbed. Apart from a few cuts and bruises he was OK though.

Leeds United

ONE of the YBO lads lives in Skipton and he'd been getting grief from the local Leeds lot. So one Saturday we were supposed to go to Bristol City but some decided to go over to Skipton instead. There were 25 of us that went over. Leeds had been playing Cardiff at home that day and word got round that they wanted a go when they got back to Keighley. So about 6pm the YBO arrived in Keighley and looked in a few pubs but they were not about. A few calls were made and it turned out the Keighley Whites were on the next train back from Leeds. To get to the platforms you have to go down these big ramps so YBO waited at the top as the train pulled in. One of ours went down and asked if they were Leeds and this stocky little cunt put him on his arse. Most of the YBO there were all about 18 but most of the Leeds lot were fellas in their 30's. The ones our age fucked off as soon as they set eyes on the City lot. So it kicked off with these blokes. They had one cunt called Windy who kept on getting decked but he kept on getting up saying: "Is that all you've got you Bradford Bastards." He must have got up about five times saying that with his face a right mess. Sirens were going off in the background and everyone fucked off. For a bloody scene that little do was bad. Everyone's trainers were red with blood. Eight of the Leeds Service Crew were laid out on the ramp either unconscious or covered in claret. But even as the police arrived you could still hear this Windy cunt shouting. He would not quit. Another do we've had with Leeds was after we'd been to a Newcastle - Rangers game in pre-season 2004. Leeds had been in Scotland playing Hibs.

There were only eight of us and these Leeds lads got on our train at York. They must have changed there. There were a few stares and stuff but nothing happened on the train. We had to get off at Leeds to change for Bradford and these Leeds lads started getting brave and mouthing it as we were all getting off. One of our lads turned round to say something back and was slashed straight across his face with a blade. Blood was pouring out. So it goes off and lads are rolling about falling on the tracks and stuff. One cunt with glasses got his head smashed on the platform edge and it bounced off. One of the lads we were with was a bit different and fuck knows why but he was wearing steel toe cap boots. I heard this crunching noise and I looked back and the specky cunt had just been given a right kick in the head. It made me shudder and we had to stop this lad taking another 10 yard run at him. We all ended up getting nicked and put in this office in Leeds Station. You could see out onto the platform. Soon after this copper came in, all panicking, and saying move us lot into a back room quickly. We're thinking what's going on here. Fuck's sake, we soon found out. A right mob of Leeds appears who had just come back from Hibs. I'd say about 200 of them. They must have heard what had happened and they were shouting, giving us grief and trying to storm the office as we were getting moved into a cleaner's cupboard. Five minutes earlier and we would have bumped into that lot. We would have been toasted. They have numbers Leeds. But to be honest I've seen nothing from them. I've never lost a do with Leeds and a lot of the older lads say the same. One of their main lads once threatened to get someone to shoot me and I later bumped into him. I was young and angry at the time so I give him it. He ended up in hospital for a few days by all accounts. Later that season Leeds stopped off in Bradford after an England game in Wales. They were not happy what had happened to one of their own lads and were putting around they were looking for me. About 20 of us had just been in town having a drink and we all went home about 10 pm as we'd been out all day watching England in the pub. I'd just got in when the phone rang and I was told Leeds had just turned up in town and get to The Queen pub.

Within ten minutes I was back in town and I was well

impressed. A good eighty had already made their way into town. By this time Leeds had been wrapped up by the police and were at the Jacobs Well pub. There were fifty of them. A lot of their main lads were in this group. There was a little bit of a do but nothing really. Fair play to them for coming, even though it was late. But I think they can count themselves lucky. The season after, thirty YBO stopped off in Leeds after we'd been to Barnsley, via twatting Leeds in Wakefield. We were boozing in the city centre there for three hours and no one came near us. Leeds had been at home that day. One Saturday afternoon we boozed all day in Headingley and phone calls were made but they never showed. You take teams as you find them and Leeds don't make much of an impression to be honest despite their reputation.

City Centre

THE YBO also got a fearsome reputation away from the football scene. More than forty would regularly hang out in the bars and clubs of Bradford city centre and this inevitably led to problems with bouncers. Many were seriously assaulted by the young gang of hooligans at work while others were beaten at their homes. Around half of the YBO have got jobs in warehouses or are plumbers etc. The rest have their own means of income. Danny says he is not proud of some of the things he has been involved with. He is now banned for life from attending any city centre bars. The YBO dominated the city with the doormen powerless to do anything about it. Some of the YBO regret not making money as a result of the grip of fear they held. The pub and club owners did not like it and neither did the police who became increasingly concerned with the gangs activities. Danny believes it was this more than football violence that led to the police wanting to crush the YBO. Here Danny reveals a typical Saturday:

"I was in town about 11 am and my phone rang. It was a pal of mine informing me Peterborough had a firm in a city centre bar. So I drop what I am doing and go for a wander to see what was going on. Right enough we find about 30 drinking in Lloyds bar. There is only seven YBO but we go in the pub for a look. Straight away I get smacked in the face but then for some reason, despite bigger numbers, the Peterborough lads back off and start throwing stuff. The YBO steam into them and these cunts arses totally went. They were cowering in the corner. What's the point coming? Later that day we decided to go for a pint in Bingley, a little town on the edge of Bradford. We had been here before and there was this bouncer who thought he was the business. He reckoned he had contacts with the Turkish Mafia. Bullshitting bastard. We go to the door and my mate was wearing an adidas hooded top. This bouncer tells him he can't come in with a hoodie . So my mate takes it off and throws it away. So he says you still can't come in. So it kicks off and this wanker bouncer shits himself and locks the door, with one of the other bouncers still outside. He is screaming inside for help, while his mate is getting battered outside. So much for the Turkish Mafia! We end up getting taxis back to Bradford and head for the Love Apple. I'm in there minding my own business when I spot this tall fella giving people grief. He must have been 6 ft 6 in tall. This fella was a real twat and had been starting on people all night. He starts bullying a kid I know who was not violent in any way. So I go to stop it and he calls me a fat cunt. Me and him have a little row and he ends up on his back. I've never seen what happened next ever before. People were lining up to kick this cunt in the head. Even women. He had been causing trouble with loads of people all night. This was like a normal Saturday for the YBO in the years from

2005-2008, three fights in one day.

Some of the lads used football as an opportunity to make money too. A load of dodgy £20 notes were doing the rounds once. We were in this pub near Chesterfield and lads were spending the notes and pocketing the change. There had been that many notes gone behind the bar the staff had to go to the local supermarket for some change. One of the lads who was being sent to the bar a lot came out shitting himself. He said the bar maid was taking ages and she knew. We then spotted her coming towards him. Oh fuck. She said: "You've forgotten your change love", and handed him a handful of pound coins and five pound notes. We all pissed ourselves laughing. Poor lass. She must have got stung for about £2,000 of dodgy notes that afternoon.

Another funny story involving those notes. A few of us were in Manchester and a mate of ours knew a lad over there. He wanted to get some sniff so he rang this Man City lad who proceeded to turn up with the gear. He was paid £240 in dodgy notes. The following day he rang my mate up and told him it was bang out of order what had happened. So my mate told him a load of bollocks that he would go to the kid's house who paid for the stuff and sort him out. The Man City lad replied: "That's a bit harsh for £20". He did not realise the rest were fake too. He must have got rid of the others without knowing. My involvement with the YBO has also led to me being splashed across a t-shirt that is for sale in a Bradford fashion shop. I was in there looking to buy a shirt when I notice myself on the front of one. It says 'Weekend Offender', and below is printed footage from my brawl with Rotherham lads which led to me being sent to prison. I was shocked and told the assistant I was the person on the shirt. He offered me the £25 shirt for a fiver."

Moving On

MY life with the Young Bradford Ointment was great fun. But there comes a time when you have to accept enough is enough. Ten of us have done jail sentences and at least another 15 have got bans. Life is not as much fun anymore but the authorities have stamped it out. The YBO only surface for certain games. About forty of us went over to Leeds with the Ointment this season (2011) for the Carling Cup Tie. But a good few had to leave the city centre early when the bans kicked in. Those who could stay ran Leeds all over. Even members of the Under Fives are on banning orders. I like my life as I'm not getting in trouble anymore but I don't feel myself somehow. I always liked the build up to it. I liked the rush it gave me. It's the best feeling I've ever had, and I've tried a lot. In a police report about me it claimed I was involved in 77 incidents of football hooliganism in some form. When I was in jail I thought that it couldn't be right so I worked it out myself. When I got to 245 I stopped. I know when my ban is up I'll go back to Valley Parade because I love the club. But for now, I'm looking at changing parts of my life. I may travel for a bit to see what's out there. I can't change the past or my time with the Young Bradford Ointment. I wouldn't want to either.

Footnote:

THE Under Fives hooligan gang hit the headlines in September 2012, when members appeared in court after a violent confrontation with Asians in Bradford. This new generation of hooligans now number over 40 with an age range of 14 -20 years of age. They are known as the 'Yoof' by regular supporters at Valley Parade and are known to have been involved in the ambushing of visiting supporters during the 2011-12 season. They seem intent on continuing the violent reputation built up by sections of Bradford City's support over decades.

Telegraph & Argus:

"Innocent members of the public, including mothers with babies in prams, were forced to flee after a gang of football hooligans clashed with Asian youths in Bradford city centre, a court heard.

Bradford Crown Court heard yesterday that people took refuge in a pub and the doors were locked to keep out the thugs. Security staff also locked up a shopping centre as the disorder swept through the centre.

Prosecutor Mehrban Nassiri told the court the disturbance happened on August 30 last year before Bradford City's home game with Sheffield Wednesday and involved a large group of white males from the Under Fives football hooligan group, who were marching into the city centre.

Trouble began when the windscreen of a Range Rover, with three Asian male occupants, was smashed. There were then violent confrontations in the street between the white youths and Asian youths.

Witnesses said both sides threw glasses and used abusive and racist language.

Mr Nassiri said the incident happened at about 5pm and there were women, children and babies in prams on the streets and people picking up relatives from work. Several people expressed their fear and sought refuge in the Commercial pub.

The scenes were captured on CCTV, which was played to the court. Among the group were Nathan Dresler, 19, James Coleman, 20, Daniel Farrar, 19, and Joseph Ewbank, 20.

All pleaded guilty to affray, except for Ewbank, who

admitted disorderly behaviour.

The court heard Farrar told a probation officer he was "proud to be a thug".

Judge Jonathan Rose told them they were a disgrace to proud football club Bradford City. He gave each of them four-year Football Banning Orders.

He said: "While it may be only Farrar who has said he is proud to be a thug, the reality is that detail applies to each of you.

"I have little doubt that each of you were quite happy to be looking for the sort of trouble that was to come. Your violent, thuggish and terrifying behaviour brought fear to those going about their legitimate business."

He sentenced Farrar, who was already subject to a Football Banning Order and had previous convictions for violence, to a total of eight months youth custody. Ewbank was sentenced to a suspended three-month sentence, with 100 hours unpaid work. Dresler and Coleman were given four-month suspended sentences, with 140 hours unpaid work.

Also before the court was 36-year-old Kadir Hussain, of Peel Square, Manningham, who admitted affray and was given a three-month suspended prison sentence.

He had been shopping for Eid, wearing traditional Asian dress, when he was racially abused and insulted and reacted by randomly throwing punches at members of the white group."

Chapter Twenty One
NEVER DULL AT HULL

HULL City supporters show hatred towards Bradford every time the teams meet.

The hooligan element of the east Yorkshire city always turned out in big numbers when the Ointment paid a visit. They treated them as their big rivals when perhaps the Bradford lads had other firms on the radar. Hull rarely brought anything of note to West Yorkshire but on their own patch they were good. On occasions the Ointment would be involved in brawls with beer swilling rugby fans and local housing estate residents.

Practically every match involving the two teams at the old Boothferry Park was marred by outbreaks of trouble in and out of the stadium. Some of those battles resulted in serious stabbing incidents. As revealed below, one Ointment lad slashed across the back at Hull came face to face with his attacker years later in a Spanish bar. The most well known clash between supporters came in 1996 when the game was halted after violent clashes on the pitch. Hull fans ran across and attacked visiting fans only to be chased back again by Bradford supporters. The violence continued outside the ground.

Much of the trouble was captured on CCTV and scores of fans were jailed.

For the Ointment, Hull City away was a fixture to look forward to.

Hull City (A)
16/02/ 85

Mark

BEFORE the game we piled off two coaches and had it with Hull near the ground. Luckily we didn't get too much grief from the police and walked round to the home end. We went in the end behind the goal and we got no trouble at all. We just jumped the turnstiles and the bloke who was taking the money was shouting:

"Oi come here."

"Come back ."

He came out of his little room and ran after a few of the lads. But he forgot to take his money so that got taken and loads more got in for nothing too. To be fair Hull's mob was actually at the opposite supermarket end so we got no trouble. The stewards and police had no idea what to do with us so we just pushed through the fence and walked around the pitch as the game was going on. We noticed our centre-half was in goal as our keeper Eric McManus had been injured. As we got to the opposite end, Hull's firm started trying to get over the fence at us. So we climbed on the fence and we were hitting each other over the top with umbrellas, fists, everything. Brilliant. This was all going on as the game was taking place. Eventually the police managed to herd us all up and put us in the away end at the side. There were 4,500 City fans and the atmosphere was both great and hostile. Not for the last time, we had more fans than Hull City.

After the match running battles between Ointment and Hull took place on the streets surrounding the ground. It was proper full on with blokes wearing Hull Rugby League tops joining in the fun. Two City fans got stabbed. One was just a regular supporter, who discharged himself from hospital to be with his wife in Bradford, who was giving birth. The other was an Ointment kid called 'Gilly' who was set on by about 20 lads. He received 30 stitches on a deep wound in his back. The local paper quoted the police as describing it as the worst violence in Hull for eight years.

Telegraph & Argus: "Labourer Simon Gill was walking towards the coaches when a gang of 20-30 started chasing him. He tripped and the gang came around him and started to kick and punch. While he was on the floor the knifeman lashed out with a Stanley blade. He got up and staggered back to the coach. He could feel his clothes beginning to soak with blood."

Hull City(A)
11/1/86

Jimmy
THIS fixture had a bit more ill feeling because the previous season two Bradford lads got slashed pretty badly. One of them a very good friend called Gilly. I don't think there was any particular plan other than get to Hull and see what happened. One thing was certain Hull knew we would be arriving, and we knew they would be waiting. The coach I was on arrived in Hull just before opening time and we headed for the pub where it kicked off the previous year called the Fiveways Hotel near the old Boothferry Park ground. However the landlord would not serve Bradford fans because of previous trouble. We ended up in this pub called the Gypsyville Tavern.We were having a drink when this cocky little wanker walked around the pub making no effort to hide the fact he was counting us. Baring in mind there is a coach load of us plus a few vans, we decided to laugh it off and just carried on drinking. When we started

leaving, these lads followed us out and started mouthing it, wanting a go. To be honest it took us a bit by surprise as there was a good 70 of us by this time. But if that's what they wanted. We got stuck in and my mate lost all his front teeth and got knocked out as these game cunts were having a go. There was no police about and it was a proper off as more and more of the cunts appeared. Some big docker type bastard came out of his house with slippers on wanting it. We were fighting for about 15 minutes and I know blades were pulled out. It was mental, you were actually stopping for a rest before getting back into it again. The fighting spilled on to a dual carriageway, traffic stopped and people were getting out to watch the fun. It was an amazing brawl. The police eventually arrived and the local nutters went back inside and we got back in our coach and vans.

Lloret De Mar, Spain
August 86

Jimmy
PAUL and Gary Dearnley, myself, Mark Bowers and Gilly were on holiday. A year before, Gilly and another lad had been carved up at Hull. He had 30 stitches across his back to close a deep wound. It was pretty much never talked about as those were the times we were living in. Besides we were on holiday and having the sort of time most lads in their late teens or early twenties would be having. The holiday is progressing and we had met lads from all over with no bother with anyone. But one night all that changed. We were in this bar and I noticed Gilly talking to this group of lads. I could see his face had changed from the chirpy lad he usually was. So I went over and he pointed at this lad and said to me:

"That's the lad who cut me."

They'd got talking and the usual where you from type conversation had gone on when this lad from Hull suddenly starts bragging about slashing a Bradford lad. The more he talked, Gilly knew it was him he was talking about. Without any hesitation I laid the nut on him and knocked his front teeth out. The other lads heard what had gone on and locked the doors of the pub. There was five of them and we gave them the hiding of their lives. The bar staff were screaming and stuff as buffets, bottles and fists rained down on these Hull bastards. In some ways we went over the top on them but what would you do in those circumstances? Poetic justice. The chances of bumping into the lad who slashed Gilly must have been astronomical and we were not going to miss the opportunity for revenge. The prick was bragging about it anyway. Later on that night we are in this other pub called the Scotch Corner when all these blokes with beards and leather jackets came in. They were part of a German biker gang known as the 'Thunderbolts'. Bowers and Paul Dearnley are playing pool and about ten of them surrounded the table. It wasn't looking good and got worse when Bowers turned round to one of them and said:

"Get out of my way you smelly bastard, I'm trying to take my shot."

I'm thinking he's just got us killed. But thank fuck they either didn't understand or saw the funny side and moved away from the pool table. Good holiday that.

Hull City (H)
25/04/87

Chris
ONE time I got dawn raided for an incident involving Hull in Bradford. It was a game which had been a bit of a non-event as Hull brought nothing. We were walking into town

and this car came past with some Hull lads mouthing it. So we sort of jogged after the car not expecting to catch it. As we were approaching the Midland Hotel we spotted a big mob of City hanging around at the bottom. One of the lads I was with started shouting :

"Get the car, it's Hull."

They clocked it and this car swerved down this ramp into Forster Square railway station which was a dead end car park at that time. The Ointment lads head down this ramp and this car is just spinning about looking for a way out. Anyhow the car got smashed to bits and the lads inside were screaming with fright. Then they just decided to run people over to make an escape and the car managed to get back up the ramp. The police were watching it all and one of them recognised me. A few days later my mate's door got kicked down by the police. When I had been nicked before I had given his address so he wasn't too happy about it. They found out where I lived and that was it. I was charged with Affray, Violent Disorder and Criminal Damage. About a dozen ended up in court and those who got dealt with by the Magistrates ended up getting six months jail which was a bit of a shock. The rest, including myself, had to go to Crown Court. We all thought we would get a two year jail sentence bearing in mind what the lads at the Magistrates got. But the judge didn't see it like that and gave us a fine and one of the first, if not the first, banning orders in the country. They had just come out and the prosecution and the judge hadn't a clue how to implement it. They were discussing whether we should be banned from athletics meetings, tennis matches, rugby that sort of thing. It took ages for them to decide to ban us from football for twenty months. We got off lightly. It was the luck of the draw in those days what sentence you would get. A few weeks later a mate of mine got 48 days jail for shouting at Leeds fans outside Elland Road.

Hull City (A)
20/04/90

Steff

EVERYONE was up for this game. Ten of us travelled down to Hull mid-week to get tickets for their seats. We'd been relegated and I suppose we wanted to go out with a bang. A few other lads had already been down and bought the tickets in bulk and unknown to us it had sent alarm bells ringing in Hull. When we bought our tickets and were walking away from the ticket office a group of lads started bouncing about and shouting at us. We thought it was Hull's boys and we were ready to steam in and started shouting come on etc. But fuck's sake it wasn't their lads, it was old bill in plain clothes and we were all lifted and charged with conspiracy. It was the height of the drugs thing as well and one of our lads had a load of gear in the car. Over 100 tickets had been bought altogether.

On the day of the match 150 went over to Hull on the train and ran them all over the city centre. They were chased out their own boozer ,The Hull Cheese, before the old bill got on top of things.

Hull managed to get off lightly that day, but Leeds celebrating winning the Division One title back in West Yorkshire, weren't so lucky. On the way back the Ointment stopped off in Leeds who had been at home to Barnsley.

We were having a go at some Leeds outside the Scarborough Pub who ran inside and bolted the doors behind them. Another mob of Leeds came out of Harlequins and flares were fired in their direction. Some of these lads stood and good luck to them but the rest scattered, easily 100 ran off. The police eventually got the Ointment back to the train station when the Service Crew came back for another go. It kicked off outside but the old bill were lifting people for fun with flares and fireworks going off.

Hull City (A)
04/05/96

Chris
WE needed to win this game to get into the play-offs in League One and interest in the game was huge. The police decided there would be less bother if the Hull home end be given to Bradford to accommodate the 7,000 travelling supporters. Obviously this did not go down well in Hull and due to previous outbreaks of violence between the two clubs, a volatile atmosphere had been created. Before the game we had about 200 knocking about in different places around the ground but the police were on top of things at this stage keeping Hull and us apart. There was a bit of running about but nothing major. As we got to the ground five of us were just hanging about waiting to go in when we spotted about thirty Hull trying to get in our end. One of our lads just flew straight in so we all ended up having a go, and to be honest we were getting ragged all over. Luckily the police were on it quick enough and the Hull lads ran off. As we got into the ground everyone was telling us Hull had ran across the pitch at us and it had just gone off big time. I remember thinking 'fucking hell we missed it'.

It would have been great had the thirty Hull got in as it would have created some right confusion with them coming across the pitch at us as well. There were a number of pitch invasions during the game, mainly when we scored, and a bit of goading Hull. But nothing like what had gone on before kick-off. I ended up getting lifted by the police during one of the pitch invasions and taken into this office. A sergeant was in there and told the copper to throw me out after he found out I was lifted for just being on the pitch.

Outside I met another Ointment lad who had been thrown out too so we went to a pub for a pint before heading back to the ground as full-time approached. We fully expected it to kick off after mounted cops and all sorts were on the pitch. Outside, Hull had come to meet us on the road down the side of the ground. Before we got there they had been bullying scarfers and getting stuck into people not wanting any bother. So we proper went for them and my mate Wibsey Scott, got his ear bitten off during the fighting. It was proper toe-to-toe and Hull were bang up for it. The coppers were just dragging people off one another and lost control initially. Lads were getting knocked out or on the floor all over the place.

Mark

ALL the City lads were meeting in a pub called the Admiral Nelson at 10 am. But by the time I got there they had all set off. To be honest I was off my head a lot at this time and taking too much gear. I was pissed off but decided to make my own way to Hull. I'd only been thumbing a lift for a few minutes when I got picked up by a mini-bus full of old City lads on the way to the match. I knew the lads were heading for a pub called Fiveways near Hull's ground and they were all drinking outside when I arrived.

There was loads of City out for this game. To be honest I was in a bad state by the start of the game. I had drunk a bottle of vodka. I was off my head too. I remember seeing them coming on to the pitch and I thought 'fuck it' I'm getting on. So I'm on the pitch and have these Nike trainers on which made me slip all over. Hull lads are coming at me from all angles. It was chaos as the Ointment started pouring onto the pitch. Individual fights were taking place with lads sparked here and there. A distress flare went flying through the air towards Hull and they began to take a beating. Before long Bradford lads were at the other end of the pitch as Hull ran off back to where they came from. Mounted police eventually restored some order. City fans made another two pitch invasions during the game but Hull were having none of it. After the game Hull were determined to rectify the embarrassment of what had happened in Boothferry Park. We clashed at the end of a dual carriageway near the ground and some of our lads say this was the best brawl they had been involved in. It was pure toe-to-toe for about forty minutes. We were fighting in gardens, in the middle of the road and on the pavement.

It was just hardcore violence and it was kicking off all over. One Hull lad got dragged down a passage by his feet. The normal police were just trying to pull fights apart and then they moved to pull some others apart. Eventually the normal police gave up and they were on each end of the dual carriageway not letting anyone through. It seemed like all of Hull had turned up. I give them credit as they did not give an inch. Their pride must have been shattered after the humiliation in the ground. They are known as the City Psychos and they lived up to their name in this battle. The riot police in their robo-cop gear arrived and that was the end of it. Lads had ears missing, broken noses, teeth missing, the lot. When we got back to Dick Delaney's Bar in Bradford, one of the lads, Smithy, had been left a message from his mum. It was simply:

"I've just seen you on ITN News."

A few weeks later the football intelligence squad came round to the same bar with a list of people. They told the landlady to tell everyone on the list to hand themselves in or they would get their doors kicked down. I didn't hand myself in but eventually got arrested. When I was sentenced in October 1996, the magistrate said to me:

"You were the first man out of the trenches and you will

go to prison for four months."

I was also banned from football for three years. I did my entire sentence in 'B' wing of Hull Prison. It was a cold dilapidated place and proper miserable.

My ban was up the week before we played Derby in 1999. People were asking me to go. I'm glad I didn't as a load went and got nicked.

The Ointment taking over Hull city centre in 1990.

Chapter Twenty Two
BADFORD V MADCHESTER

CLASHES with the Manchester clubs have been sporadic over the years. In the case of Man City there was a flurry of games in the 80's and 90's in what is now the Championship. Games against Man Utd were restricted to the isolated cup match and Bradford City's two seasons in the Premier League at the turn of the Millennium. However, despite not being a regular feature on the fixture list, games with the two giants across the Pennines have not been without incident. In fact, some of the matches have resulted in serious outbreaks of violence. In 2001 Manchester United's Red Army turned up in huge numbers after being turned over in Bradford the year before. As for Man City, many Ointment lads rate these lads as they always turn up looking for it.

Manchester City (A)
23/04/88

Phil
THE coach driver dropped us off in Moss Side estate and what a fucking dump that was. But well dodgy too. Some of the lads had come over by train so there were only about 50 of us but it was all good lads. It was a few hours before kick-off and people were staring at us as we made our way through the estate. It was a very leery atmosphere. You had

a sense that something was about to happen and although I trusted my pals I did think there wasn't enough of us. We managed to get to the Maine Road ground after what seemed like ages unscathed. We didn't see any lads at all until outside the stadium when there was a bit of running about but the police on horses were keen as fuck hitting people with their truncheons. One of the Man City lads actually lived in Bradford and he said he would sort something out after the match. After the game about 100 of us start going on a walk and this shop-hopper style bus came past with a few Man City on it. They are giving it large as it goes past at speed. But further up the road it stopped at lights. We ran up and started rocking the fucker and it's about to go over when these lads get off. Fair play to them they had a go but we outnumbered them. The police arrived and again they were smacking everyone with truncheons. I felt sorry for the shoppers on the bus as they were in shock. The police were chasing us about in vans for a bit after.

Manchester United (H)
25/03/00

Steff

THE first time we played them in the Premier League I thought they were wank. We had hundreds out. Probably one of the biggest mobs we've ever had. Lads I had not seen for years were out and about in town. It was the game everyone had looked forward to the most. Manchester had lads turning up on the trains and we were having skirmishes around town but they were shit. They had different mobs of about 30-50 turning up and they were just getting scattered. One of their main boys is a kid called Coco and his lot got done near St George's Hall. One group we had it with were from Oldham. This was good enough toe-to-toe on Sunbridge Road. But even one of these knobs was in the back of a police car later pointing out people he thought had nicked his hat. As I say there were little battles going off here and there but the feeling was of a huge anti-climax. They hadn't come in one big mob as we expected. They probably thought coming to Bradford would be no big deal. They were wrong. However, they wouldn't make the same mistake the following season.

Chris
AFTER the match we were walking down Manor Row in the city centre when we came across a mob of Mancs who were mouthing it off and seemed up for it. But there were a load of cops about. In the confusion of trying to keep us apart they ended up putting some of the Ointment in the Mancs escort. Elbows started flying and it wasn't long before the whole escort erupted. A copper attached to the football intelligence unit sussed us out and separated us from the Mancs. The bastards then set the dogs on us and one of the lads got his leg ripped to pieces.

Manchester United (H)
13/01/01

Steff
THEY came big time for this game. There must have been 400 of them and they were all lads. The best firm ever to come to Bradford. We had another very good mob out. We'd heard in the morning United lads had given Leeds a pasting in Rochdale. The Service Crew were on their way to Man City. The old bill were on it and as soon as the main mob arrived in Bradford they were wrapped up and escorted to the ground. We had it with a few smaller groups before

the game but nothing major. The real fun started inside Valley Parade. The away fans were given two sections of the stadium in opposite ends of the ground. One of which was in between the Kop and the main stand with no real segregation. So you had a situation where 2,300 Man Utd supporters were right in the middle of City fans. It kicked-off and there were lads fighting over a small wall and climbing in each other's end. Something was going off throughout the game. After the match a load of us were waiting outside the ground and picking a few off but there were loads of old bill. We made our way towards town as we knew their lads would have to get back to the Interchange. About 50 of us were waiting on the junction of Manningham Lane and Manor Row. We were not really expecting to get anything as the police would be all over the Manchester lads. Then we spotted this wall of black coming along Manningham Lane. It looked very, very impressive. This mob, at least 400 strong, is coming right at us. I looked around and I knew the lads I was with wouldn't budge. We were saying to each other let's have it with the cunts. So they come and we are at it with them giving as good as we got but they had too many. They were all around us and it came on top. But we never backed off and they know that. We got done but we had a go against a mob that would have taken anyone in the country. The old bill came and everyone fucked off. More and more of us lot started to get it together and all the way back to the Interchange we were at it with Manchester who were now in a huge police escort. Some of ours managed to get in amongst them and were fighting inside the escort. They brought a massive firm over and sometimes you just have to take your hat off. But even Manchester United lads know they can't take a trip to Bradford lightly.

Football Intelligence :
"Bradford City v Manchester United 13/01/01 - Premier League.
During the game rival supporters clashed with each other inside the stadium. Several fights erupted and there was spitting and verbal abuse between the supporters. Several arrests were made. At the end of the match there were sporadic outbursts of fighting between the rival groups. A section of the Manchester United supporters made their way to the city centre. This group fought with anyone who challenged them on route. As the Manchester group passed through Centenary Square individual fights occurred between rival groups."

Manchester City (A)
16/12/01

Dean
IT was a Sunday game and about 80 of us went on the train. We walked from the town centre up to Maine Road and chased a few off but nothing much. One of our lads was friendly with a Man Utd lad and he took us on the route. It was about five miles to the fucking ground. We got to the Parkside Pub where they have a drink and they were all looking outside at us. The coppers were not expecting us at all. They were arguing with each other:
"Where has this lot come from?" and stuff like that. By the time we had got to the ground the game had already started. But instead of letting us in, the police escorted us all the way back into town and put us on the first train to Bradford. Nothing happened but I was fucking knackered.

Manchester City (H)
08/03/02

Chris

I RATE Manchester City as they always brought a decent mob over to Bradford. They were never scared of dotting about in different places looking for it. An old bastard with this lot turned out be good at martial arts and gave me a Kung-Fu kick, breaking one of my ribs. I also ended up with a scar on my head after it came on top and I got left before the game. To this day I have no idea what weapon was used on my head but it had to be some sort of blade. After the match a good few Manchester lads were in a pub called the Rams Revenge in Bradford city centre. Bit by bit Ointment lads started to arrive as word got round the 'Guvnors' were in town. You could feel the tension in the pub as the Man City lads, who were all sat down, became aware the pub was beginning to fill up with Bradford. Some were even holding empty bottles, no longer interested in going to the bar for a drink. You could see they were worried but too proud or whatever to try and do a runner. They knew they had made a mistake by going for a drink in Bradford. Eventually the tension snapped and the Ointment got stuck into them with a load of Man City getting CS gas sprayed in their faces. It was a swift but very brutal attack with a good few 'Guvnors' getting battered with chairs, tables and bottles. But with the Rams Revenge being in the city centre, the police arrived within minutes and it was all over.

Chapter Twenty Three
STRANGE DAYS

ON occasions the Ointment has got more than it bargained for when travelling across the country. From rows with violent families, village idiots, miraculous escapes from road traffic accidents and out of space shenanigans at Hereford. Here is a selection of some of the stories that don't quite fit in anywhere else.

York City (A)
25/03/95

Chris
WHAT stands out about this was not want went on with York but an incident with the old bill. We were on our way back and stopped at this off-licence to get some beer. We were all in a box van and everyone got out. Some of our lot emptied the place and paid for fuck all. Everyone got back in and start getting stuck into the booze. Ten minutes down the road we hear sirens and the van gets pulled over. We could hear the police outside and they started trying to lift the door up at the back. But as they are pulling it up, we are pulling it back down again. This seemed to be going on for ages and you could hear they were getting angry outside. At one point they got the door up so far that they tried to get a dog in but failed. We were shouting abuse and it was

getting to be a battle of wills. Eventually they managed to drag a lad called Cody, from Batley, out of the van. They fucking battered him. You could hear the kicking he was getting outside and we thought we're fucked too. They shouted in that we should leave the van two at a time. So I thought fuck it we can't stay here all night. So I said to Greengates Scotty to come with me as I knew that if it did kick-off with the police he would have a go back with me. We were sure we were walking into a battering. But to our surprise when we jumped out they were alright with us and brought us to this Transit police mini-bus thing. We couldn't believe we didn't get touched. But another lad didn't get off so lightly and they broke his ankles by slamming the door down on them. Nobody put their hands up to thieving from the shop so they ended up letting us go.

Shrewsbury Town (A)
23/11/85

Chris

I HIRED a box van to go to Shrewsbury and there were 17 in the back. We got there no problem but as I drove through a roundabout in Shrewsbury, I heard this bang. I looked through the rear view mirror and there was nothing there. The box with all the lads inside had gone. The box had fucking fallen off. The chassis and the cab were alright so I pulled up and all three of us from the front ran back down the road. To be honest I was worried. The box was on its side and I thought someone may have died. We managed to pull the door open. Everyone was still laid down apart from the General who was stood up telling everyone:

"It's alright I can't smell smoke, it's not on fire."

He caused more panic than if he'd said nothing. Everyone got out and thankfully no one was seriously injured apart from a few bruises and the odd head wound. The police arrived and everyone got themselves sorted. While the rest went down the road to a pub I had to hang about and give a statement. I'm in the back of this patrol car giving my details to this copper and a message came over the radio about a fight at this pub. The copper quit asking me anything and turned on his ignition saying:

"That's where your mates have gone."

So we sped off and after a minute pull up at this pub. And there it is, all our lot smashing the place up and brawling in the car park while I'm sat in this police car watching it. More police arrived and our lot fucked off. Anyhow after a few minutes this copper got back in the car and told me we'd better go back to the station otherwise he'd be dealing with this sort of stuff all afternoon. He was a moaning twat.

"I've been in the force twenty years and this is only the second time I've had to draw my truncheon," he said.

"The other time was when Leeds came here. What is it with you Yorkshire bastards?"

After the game of course we had no van to get home. Another one of the lads had also brought a box van with about the same number in it. So he told us to get in his. The thing was heaving and very illegal. We had to stand up shoulder to shoulder and every time we went round a corner we held our breath. We eventually got as far as Oldham. I have no idea why we went to Oldham but we ended up getting pulled over by a copper on a motor bike. He's walking round tapping on the side of the van. Ten of us got out and the policeman says:

"Have all you lot come from in there?"

He had no idea there was another 30 still inside. He gets on his radio and starts asking for back up so everyone piled out. His eyes were popping out of his head. He must have thought it was the Tardis. We all ran off up Oldham High Street and we got a bus to Huddersfield and then eventually home.

Strange day that.

Cambridge United (A)
05/12/87

Chris

I WAS on a coach of really good lads who were involved in this incident after a game at Ipswich. We had a few scuffles with Ipswich before the game and during it we chased them out of their seats. I got a 50 pence piece straight in the eye for my troubles. After the match we decided to stop off in Cambridge. To be honest we never expected any trouble. It was not long after there had been a lot of publicity about Chelsea being attacked by a mob of Cambridge lads led by someone known as 'The General'. But other than that we thought the town would be full of student types and we just went for a beer. Most of the night everything was quiet and we had all split up going to different bars. We arranged to meet back at the coach at 11 pm, and as we all drifted back people were going on about these lads saying we should head for a club called Munroe's. We were told this is where the local hard men went and if we were looking for a bit of trouble we would get it here. We told our driver that some of our lads were not on the coach and were in this nightclub called Munroe's. He set off and pulls up right outside this club. We all piled off the coach and walked to the club where the bouncers tried to stop us. One of our main lads called Andy sparked one of the bouncers straight out and there was a big scuffle at the door. Three of us got in at first, me, Javo and Paul Durrant. We headed down the stairs where we spotted these lads who had been telling us this was the place to go for a fight in Cambridge so we had it with them. It wasn't long before the rest of the club realised there was only three of us and started attacking us, including women. It was chaos and we ended up being hit with anything that wasn't bolted down. Somehow we managed to get back up the stairs where there was a scene of carnage with all the bouncers sparked out on the floor and the place smashed to pieces. As we got back on the coach the whole club came out for a go and some of our windows were smashed. I remember the trip home was fucking freezing. There was snow coming through the windows all the way from Cambridge.

Hereford United (A)
08/12/79

General
FIFTY of us were in this pub in the town centre when these skinheads came in all wearing black bomber jackets. Most of them had dyed blonde hair. They were bumping into people and looked like trouble. When about 20 of them got in trouble started with beer glasses flying. We backed these silly cunts onto the High Street. Just across from the pub there was a Star Wars convention and there were lines of people dressed up as Chewbacca and Princess Leia. It was like being on another planet rather than a small English town as we were laying into these blonde kids. They eventually ran off and the old bill arrived. The police hadn't a clue and told us they were going to escort us to the ground for our own safety. As we looked back on the High Street it looked like a war zone with tables, chairs, and bottles smashed all over the place. To cap it off, stunned Star Wars fans in their mental uniforms watched as we headed over the hill.

Port Vale (A)
24/09/83

Gen

A FEW van loads of us had been on the outskirts of town having a drink and not really expecting anything to be honest. As we set off walking to the ground we saw this gang heading towards us and they started mouthing it. There were about 20 of us and mostly young lads. As this group got closer we noticed they had real big bastards with them and I thought we could have a bit of bother. They looked like local hard men rather than football supporters. There were loads of milk crates lined up along this street so we got them and started throwing the bottles at these lads as they got closer. It went off and one of our lads smacked this kid who gave his head a right bang on a wall as he went down. He never moved and I thought that he was dead. He just lay completely motionless. There was a bit more scuffling and we fucked off. In the ground the police were walking in front of the City supporters and looking at the crowd through binoculars. They then came in and started nicking some of our lads who had been at the fight. We were getting worried as we thought this lad had indeed snuffed it. He was in a coma for a bit but thankfully did not die and the lads who got nicked were only fined. The kid who punched the lad was never arrested for it. It turned out that we had been fighting members of a local nutter family called the McGraths. A few months later we played Port Vale at home and all the lads are in the seats as usual. Just before kick-off these blokes came in amongst us all and started spitting at everyone.

"Come on you cunts we're the McGraths" one of them shouted.

For fuck's sake. I had spit all over my new Tacchini so

I cracked one of the cunts in the face. They got a kicking but they were real mad cunts.

Ilkeston
20/04/87
Badger

WE'D been to Derby and flares and stuff were going off as we clashed with the DLF before the game. Most of us had gone in a fleet of vans and mini-buses and I remember a few lads turned up in a Robin Reliant. There would have been 150 or so of us altogether. We always turned up for Derby. I was in the back of an old meat van that had a few small holes in the side so we could breath. After the game about 50 of us stopped off in the village of Ilkeston. First thing I remember was the thud of bricks hitting the side of the van as it stopped. I got out of the back into a scene of chaos. All the vans had emptied and groups of lads were hitting lumps out of each other. What the hell? These big guys were piling out of pubs and coming at us. I remember one old guy painting the last bit of fence in his garden before it was completely dismantled by City lads wanting the wood for weapons. It was a Bank Holiday Monday and it seemed we had pulled up in front of the roughest pub in the area with the local hard men all outside pissed. This huge body builder ripped his shirt off and nobody could get him down. Punches were flying into him but he did not flinch. One lad called Baz was having a fencing match with the guy. I had done some rugby in my youth and came up behind him and tackled him to the ground. But these guys were well game. I could not believe what was going on. We heard after they were a mix of Forest and Derby. This sleepy town had turned into a war zone and this is how it was described in the local press the following day. I got to know a lad from the area years later and he remembered the incident well. He knew the big guy who would not go down. He told me that he broke his neck and died after taking a bet to run into a brick wall!

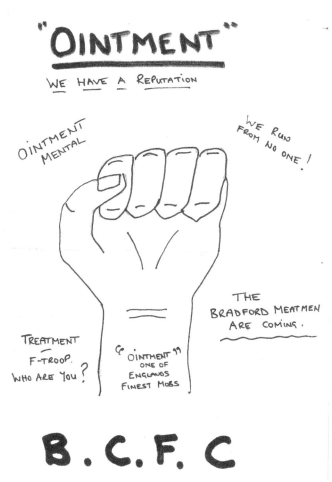

HUNDREDS of these leaflets were posted on street and tube station walls in south-east London in the weeks leading up to a game at The Den in 1982. TV, newspaper and radio appeals were made for calm.

Chapter Twenty Four
THANKS FOR THE MEMORIES

TO mention every firm who the Ointment has had a row with over the years would require another book. There are scores of hooligan gangs who turned out for Bradford that didn't quite make the final draft this time. Some have sprung surprises and had a real go. These would include Blackburn, Doncaster, Hartlepool, Darlington, Bristol Rovers ,Walsall and many more. Below are some who did manage to make it. These are recollections of tussles with rival thugs that have stuck in the memory of some of the Ointment's most senior members.

Lincoln City (A)
30/10/82

Paul Whitehead
FIVE van loads went down for this game and Lincoln had a little bit of a reputation at the time. In those days before mobile phones, etc it was just by bumping into the opposing firm that things would happen. We found them in a pub called the Swiss Cottage. They came running out with pool cues as we walked passed. I remember one lad ran back in and accidently poked his mate in the eye with a cue. The pub got smashed up and a Lincoln fan got stabbed. After

the game all the van drivers got arrested and we were all taken in for questioning over the stabbing incident. They kept a couple of our lads in for questioning including a London based Ointment lad. The rest of us were put back in the vans and escorted all the way from Lincoln back to Bradford.

Plymouth Argyle (H)
23/08/86

Phil

THIS game stands out in the memory. It was the first game of our second season at Odsal Stadium, and just four months before City would return to Valley Parade. It was a big game for Plymouth as they had just been promoted to the Second Division. Hundreds of them had travelled to Bradford through the night and had been hanging around town from 6 am. Most of them we came across were scarfers but they were well oiled. They were lying pissed up in shop doorways and so on. A few pubs had been trashed and one in Wibsey had all its walls smeared in shit by pissed up Plymouth fans. This lot were biker, heavy metal types. It was weird. We had not expected any of this and as we started meeting up, different lads were talking about bumping into Plymouth at different times of the morning. A few hours before kick-off we managed to sort ourselves out a bit and had given some Plymouth a kicking outside the Admiral Nelson on Manchester Road. One big lad with curly hair was out cold. By the time we got to Wibsey there was about 80 of us. As we got near Wibsey High Street about 300 Plymouth came charging down the road at us. A mix of scarfers and lads. We backed off down Wibsey Bank and regathered at The Woodman Pub car-park. They came charging down the hill, some of the cunts

were in fancy dress too and we had it with them. I lost count
of how many lads from both sides were getting put down or
covered in blood. Chairs from the pub were being used as
weapons and it was possibly the best do I've been involved
in. I rate Plymouth a lot after this although they've brought
nothing since. It was a big game for them and the whole
town seemed to turn up for it. We were outnumbered against
a set of supporters well up for it. After the old bill arrived
we jumped over the railings on Manchester Road near the
Red Lion Pub.   On the floor, semi-unconscious and
mumbling "Bradford Bastards," was the same curly haired
Plymouth lad who had been knocked out at the Admiral
Nelson. The poor cunt had been smacked at the Red Lion
too. Funny.

West Brom (H)
18/02/89

Steff
THE thing that sticks in the mind about this is how much
stuff can be thrown out of a bar. We were in the Bradford
Arms when we heard West Brom were up the road in the
Belle Vue. There are about 30 of us taking a walk up to see
what they had brought. We walked inside and they had a
very good set of lads in around the pool room. Within
seconds the place goes up and they were throwing
everything at us. We had no choice but to back off and to be
honest we were getting a hiding. We got outside and they
are tooled up to fuck with bottles, pool cue and balls. They
had even smashed the bandits and pool table to pieces and
were throwing bits of those at us. The police arrived and for
a change left us and started nicking some West Brom lads.
One City lad had jumped over the bar when it kicked off.
Later he came outside. The pub is trashed, police all over

the place, and he asks: "Is it finished yet Steff?"

Some West Brom eventually got jail for this. The pub closed down for good shortly after. I see one of the West Brom lads at Rangers games now and we get on great.

Grimsby Town (A)
15/09/90

Steff

THIS was one of the best days out on the road for football violence. For a good four hours we were at it with Grimsby in the streets and on the beach in Cleethorpes .The police couldn't keep a lid on it as running battles went on all over the place, while at the same time shops were being looted. Lads were fighting while carrying suits and all sorts of stuff under their arms. They even had a Chinese lad with them who thought he was Bruce Lee. And he fucking nearly was.

The 'Welcome To Cleethorpes' sign was hanging off after being pelted with bricks and beer bottles and it summed up the day perfectly. It all started when we were in a pub in Cleethorpes having no bother at all. A couple of our lads had been for a wander and bumped into some Grimsby who said they had a mob out for us. But we didn't give a fuck what they had to be honest. We had come over in a coach, vans and cars and it was a cracking day by the sea. So we are in this boozer when the old bill arrived and ordered the landlord to get us out. He was sound with us but they insisted we left. Fucking stupid decision. So 80-100 of us leave this pub and start to split up to give the old bill the run around. It was during this walkabout Grimsby appeared. They came charging across a bowling green towards us. It was a proper pitched battle and they were well up for it. The numbers were pretty even at this point and people were going down on both sides. One of our lads was hitting them with a bucket and spade. More and more of our lads started to head towards the front and we backed Grimsby, whose mob is called Cleethorpes Beach Patrol, onto the beach. The police are running around like headless chickens and they didn't have the manpower to stop it. Some of our lads and Grimsby kids had spotted other opportunities during the chaos and started robbing shops.

The fun and games continued on the beach with Grimsby having a real go. The police charged one group with truncheons one minute and then turned around and did the same to the other. The fighting continued on and off the beach for what seemed like hours before the police managed to get us wrapped up. They had managed to get a load of dog vans. The police escorted us to the ground and it seemed to take fucking ages. Grimsby kept on coming for another go and fights kept on breaking out. A tough Gypsy lad with us called Gervais smashed two coke cans into this poor cunt's face who was covered in claret. We eventually got in the ground about 20 minutes after kick-off. After the game some lads who had gone to get the car home said Grimsby had loads waiting but were being forced back by the police. Fair play to Grimsby they were game as fuck. It was a brilliant day. A few of ours got arrested and met some of them in court and they were bang sound.

Coventry (A)
18/03/00

Phil
TWO coaches of us set off early from Buttershaw so we could be in Coventry by the time the pubs opened. One of our lads was on speaking terms with members of Coventry's mob 'The Legion', and they had warned us there would be a welcoming committee out for us. We were boozing in the

city centre and apart from running a few around the place they looked to have no lads at all. About 2pm I was sat on a wall outside this pub when a good 80 Coventry appeared in the car-park. I got smacked in the face and fell off the wall. Another kid booted me in the face and I could taste blood in my mouth. Thank fuck our lot came out of the pub and for a few minutes it was proper toe-to-toe in the car park. The old bill arrived and broke everything up. After the game we managed to give the police the slip and went looking for Coventry who appeared in a children's playground. This was fucking bizarre as people were getting decked on the roundabout while swings were being used as missiles. It was like a comedy film. Coventry did not stand this time and one of their lads took a terrible kicking and I thought he might be dead. The coppers were out with the batons and got stuck into us big time. One of our lads nicked a phone off one of the Coventry lads and on the way home it was passed around for everyone to use. One silly cunt rang up threatening to do this and that the next time we were in town. We did go back to Coventry the year after but were all wrapped up by the old bill and detained until well after the match.

Grimsby Town (H)
31/01/09

Steff

I WAS in Huddersfield and a got a call from one of the lads to say Grimsby had been on the phone and they were bringing a firm over. Many teams in the lower leagues chose Bradford as the big day out of the season. We'd been over there a few months before on a Friday night. Eight of us were in a bar when about 30 of their lads came in. They were alright with us as they could have taken the piss.

They'd already been at it with a load of Young Bradford Ointment (YBO) who were put back on the coach to Bradford. So I got a lift back from Huddersfield and head for the Bedford Arms where the Ointment had told Grimsby they would be waiting. We hung around a couple of hours but they never showed so we all fucked off. We then a get a call saying they had just arrived at the Bedford. So we go back and there they all are outside, about 50 of them. So it goes off and they are giving as good as they get with no one moving an inch on either side. I recognised one of their boys from Rangers games. The old bill came and that was the end of that. A bit later this Grimsby lad from Rangers is on the phone to me asking how we thought it went and stuff. I said fair play to him and his mates for a good little row.

Nobody came out on top and it was bit like an 80's do. So that was that. An hour later the lad rings again calling me a cunt and stuff saying they had been put on a bus and it had been attacked with windows getting smashed and stuff. I knew fuck all about it at the time. I later found out the YBO had done it.

Exeter City (A)
14/03/09

Phil
A COACH load of us set off from Bradford at midnight and by the time we arrived in Exeter at 5 am we were all pretty much pissed or off our heads. There were some good lads on the bus and a few very old heads. But it was more of a piss up trip than anything else. When we got there we split up looking for pubs and got no trouble. After the match I was drinking outside this pub called the Duke of William in the town centre when one of our lads phoned saying Exeter's firm known as the 'Sly Crew', were giving it to

some of our lot. We headed down the street and first thing I saw were these two giant cunts at the front knocking our lads over for fun. It seemed the whole town had come out for us and we heard later it was chavs from a local housing estate. They were well up for it. When the numbers evened up a bit Exeter backed off but still it was a good do until the police dog handlers separated us. Some of them were tooled up with pool balls in socks and coshes. It turned out Exeter had got stuck into some of our scarfers as well, including an old man and his grandson.

The End